Healing With Dreams

HEALING WITH DREAMS

Empower Yourself with the Law of Attraction & Create a New Reality

George Rhatigan

This book is a revised and updated addition to the book "Dreams Secret Language of the Soul", written by George Rhatigan and first published in 1996 by Salmon Publishing, a division of Auburn House.

Illustrations by George Rhatigan & Máire Herbert.

Healing with Dreams: Empower yourself with the Law of Attraction to Create your New Reality / George Rhatigan & Sharon Ní Chuilibín

ISBN: 978-1-7395917-0-0

Design & Layout by Sharon Ní Chuilibín

Typesetting via Pressbooks using the "Dillard" Theme.

Published by www.soulcompass.ie

Contents

List of Illustrations ix
Acknowledgements xi
Preface xiii
Foreword xxv
Introduction 1

1. What are Dreams, how do they Work? 15
2. Dreams and the Law of Attraction 25
3. Four Rules of Dream Interpretation 41
4. Understanding your Dreams 47
5. Techniques for Dream Interpretation 57
6. Techniques for Dream Interpretation 63
7. Heal yourself by Changing your Dreams 71
8. Aspects of Dreams, Dreaming and Life 77
9. How Can I Remember my Dreams? 147
10. The Power of Mantras 151
11. Different Kinds of Dream 157
12. Examples of Healing Success 171
13. What happens when you Sleep? 187
14. Trinity of the Mind 191

15. Hypnosis, Meditation and Dreams 197

16. Locations and Other Symbols 205

16. Chakras, Chakra Healing and Colors 221

17. The Meaning and Use of Numbers 245

19. The 'Personality' of Illness 253

18. Personality Types: Roles People Play 267

19. Steps to Avoid Chronic Ailments 275

22. Healing Techniques 283

23. The Secret of Success 293

24. Spiritual Healing 299

20. The Three States of Awareness 305

26. The Wishing Man 311

27. My Cosmic Order 319

My Law – Tieme Ranapiri 321

Further Reading 325

Other Books by this Author 327

LIST OF ILLUSTRATIONS

Fig.1. Guide, Shadow Self & Healing Agent (Pg. 24)

Fig.2 : The Magic Mirror of Dreams (Pg. 62)

Fig.3: Techniques to remember Dreams (Pg. 148)

Fig. 4: Astral Travel during Sleep (Pg. 187)

Fig. 5: Your eight hours of sleep: four two-hour sleep cycles. (Pg. 190)

Fig. 6: Energy movement as we sleep. (Pg. 196)

Fig. 7: Healing techniques. (Pg. 301)

Fig. 8: Cover Image "The Wishing Man". (Pg. 314)

Figures 1-6, illustrated by George Rhatigan. Figure 7 by Marie Herbert. Additional image processing by Lughnasa Tornoczi-Philbin

ACKNOWLEDGEMENTS

I would like to acknowledge the work of Edgar Cayce and The Association for Research and Enlightenment in formulating my first understanding of dreams. I would also like to thank my mentors, Maura Lundberg and Paddy Mc Mahon who first encouraged my interest in channeling and psychic development.

My thanks to Gary Birney my good friend, for his never-ending support and inspiration, and to Olga Fraser for her meticulous work in editing the original manuscript.

Thanks to Sharon Ní Chuilibín who has assisted me in bringing this book to you its present form and provided insights & advice on the journey. Thanks also to the psychic artist Marie Herbert who provided many of the illustrations in this book, and to Irene Bermingham for her support and practical assistance in promoting it.

A special word of thanks to Brendan O' Callaghan for his encouragement and inspiration.

I would also like to acknowledge and thank my guides, Brother John, Joseph, the Native American Standing Bear & Hilarious. They all have their skills and talents. Brother John helps me with the Tarot, Joseph helps me with dreams, and Standing Bear helps me with Absent Healing & Channelling. Hilarious helps me with having a sense of humour.

Finally, my thanks to you dear reader. It is in your hands now to bring this work into your lives, and into a world that is so much in need of healing.

PREFACE

Imagine talking about dreams to a group of people, for example standing in a bus queue. Your companions are from all walks of life: male, female, young, old, healthy, ill, wealthy, poor, etc. They all have issues, interests and worries. And they all dream. You tell them that whatever concerns them during the day will, inevitably become the subject of their dreams at night. These nightly dramas can contain information, guidance and healing on all aspects of their lives. A dream is designed to be inter-active like a computer. You can re-enter and change it using a short meditation at any time after having it. In this way you can get your dream to explain itself and receive many benefits. You will learn all of this and more within the pages of this book.

Most men's dreams involve work issues so it will not be long before someone, usually a man, will say: "Dream Interpretation may be an interesting subject but how can it help me with my business?". Dreams about work issues usually involve traffic ("trafficking" = business) in the street and commercial vehicles e.g. a new white van might indicate a new business idea or project. By learning the language of dreams, re-entering them and interacting with the characters involved, the dreamer can be informed of new ideas and commercial opportunities. For example, the inventor of the sewing machine got the idea of putting the hole in the pointed end of the needle from a dream about knights carrying lances similarly pierced. If, in the dream the dreamer or a vehicle is late or in the wrong place, then the dreamer may be missing out on opportunities by not being in the right place at the right time. A new articulated truck might suggest a flexible, intuitive/logical approach to business. The dream might also indicate how he could benefit by learning how to attract wealth and abundance – using the Law of Attraction which dreams can help us all with.

A woman e.g. might ask: "Why can't I find love and why do all my relationships fail?" In over forty years of experience, I have found that women's dreams are more likely to be about relationships – e.g. how to get the best out of the present one or allow a new one to manifest itself. You may believe that love at first sight happens entirely by chance, but dreams indicate differently. We are destined to meet partners, friends and enemies. These encounters are carefully and cleverly choreographed in our dreams. You wake up one morning with the idea that you should go to a certain place at a certain time. Your partner-to-be gets a similar message and you both meet, apparently by chance. You may both feel as if you have known the other person all your life; you have, but it was in a previous incarnation. The result may be instant love or hate. If, however, you are not a spontaneous person you may, like the businessman above, dismiss the thought and miss the pre-ordained meeting. Look out for dreams where "funny things happen on the way to a wedding". In such a dream the taxi may be late, you miss the bus or train connection or you arrive unsuitably dressed. Such dreams may indicate a possible new relationship but they may also concern themselves with what hang-ups or issues you take into relationships. Two of anything (pairs) can indicate the pattern of your relationships e.g. two ill-matched shoes, a cat and a dog and so on. You may find yourself, e.g. walking a dog on a tight leash. Are you too controlling of yourself or partners ?

Let's say a woman from the queue asks: "I am on

chemotherapy for cancer in my uterus. What can dreams do to speed up my recovery?" Health warnings are common in dreams. They appear years before the physical manifestation of the illness. They often indicate how a negative belief system about some aspect of the body or it's functioning can create stress, toxic energy and illness. If the advice of the dream is followed, the predicted illness can often be avoided. If you already have the illness, your dreams will help you to fight it, naturally, having consulted a doctor. Dreams often do this by creating a scenario in a symbolic part of the house (your body in dream language), in which your illness is given a shape and size to help you to deal with it.

The woman's question above reminds me of the dream of another woman who came to me with a similar problem. "The dream takes place in a dirty, cluttered bedroom. A family of rats has taken up residence in the bed and are eating into the furniture. An exhausted, fat terrier dog lies on it's back nearby, panting". The bedroom represents her view of sexuality ("it's dirty"), and the bed indicates the state of her reproductive system as a result of this belief. The hatred and disrespect she subconsciously holds for this aspect of her functioning is creating illness. Cancer cells can appear as negative life forms e.g. rats, sharks, foxes, criminals, etc. The terrier dog whose job it is to kill rats represents her immune system which is exhausted by stress and overwork. I helped her to re-enter the dream using a short meditation (described in the book). I told her to get rid of the clutter (clear her mind) and clean the carpet as it represents her understanding (ie. under where she stands) or opinion of sexuality. I instructed her to talk to the rats and ask them what memories of her childhood are "eating her" – ie. making her reject her feminine functioning and sub-consciously self-destruct. Negative incidents, attitudes, and beliefs associated with her parents came to mind which she re-evaluated and released. She was given guidance on how to re-activate her immune system (the dog). She regularly repeated this process and the cancer soon went into remission.

If your child has a problem, whether it is cancer, anxiety, depression or whatever, you can naturally, feel helpless. A typical question might be; "My teenage son no longer speaks to me. He will not leave his bedroom. I have no idea what is going on in his head. What can I do?" You may think you understand and love your children, but ask yourself how well your parents understood and loved you, and even if they did, how good was the communication between you and them? Dreams are door openers as to what people are really thinking. By talking to your family in a meaningful way and sharing dreams at the breakfast table, you can come to understand them on a deeper level. Your son may be experiencing bullying, or being abused. His cancer may be due to something that happened at his birth that left him with the sub-conscious belief system that he was not acceptable or loved.

All the issues of the people discussed above arise from a painful incident or incidents which caused them to sub-consciously feel that they or some aspect of their functioning were unacceptable. Therefore, removing this negative, unhelpful belief and helping them to accept themselves can be very helpful. You, as a parent or friend can do this if you choose. A mother came to me to help get her teenage daughter Anne off her addiction to medically prescribed drugs. The child was once happy and outgoing but now she refused to leave the house. She had to wait three months to see a psychotherapist. This person diagnosed clinical depression and prescribed medication. Anne became addicted and would not go to school without her drugs. Her studies suffered. I asked her for a dream but she could not recall any. I decided to use memories instead. This is a process which I call the' 3 M's' (See Chapter 21). In a similar fashion to re-entering and changing dreams, the process of 3 M's allows you to recall a relevant memory and change that. She related how, some years previously she was nominated as best pupil in the school. The prize was to be given to her in church by the bishop in a ceremony attended by her classmates and parents. As she went up to receive the prize she was terrified and defecated in her knickers. She ran from the church and would not leave her house.

The healing mentioned above involves a five minute meditation and then (1) Memory (in this case the incident in church), (2) Meaning (understanding what she was doing to her life as a result) and then (3) Movement. This part varies with the individual but in Anne's case I got her to look at the incident as if she is looking at it in a cartoon movie. All the characters, including the bishop, dance around to silly music and talk like cartoon characters. The film is then destroyed. Needless to say the therapy worked. She stopped taking the drugs, with medical advice, and she was soon back to her happy, healthy self.

Dreams, even from the ordinary 'man in the street' often contain great wisdom and insight as well as visions of past, present and possible future. This gives rise to questions such as; where does this wisdom and information come from? What do dreams say about my birth and purpose in life? What latent talents, gifts, or abilities do I or my family have? Once again, I remind you that dreams, like computers, are designed to be interactive. If you want to know the answer to any question, write it on a piece of paper and put it under your pillow. You will be answered in your dreams. However, you may have to learn how to remember and understand these nightly messages. You may also have to keep an open mind, because the answer when it comes may only be understood within a spiritual or philosophical context that may be unfamiliar to you. Dreams will often refer to e.g. reincarnation, your Life Purpose, what spiritual gifts, powers, talents and abilities you have even if they are latent in present time and much more of what may not be part of your culture, background or education. Indeed, it is not uncommon for a person who has no knowledge of spiritual gifts to dream of practicing "hands-on" or, distant healing, channeling, clairvoyance, etc. This usually means that it may be a part of the dreamer's Life Purpose to develop and use such abilities. Naturally, understanding and re-entering such dreams and using the powers in the dream state can make it easier to develop them in the waking state. This can also apply to any talent or ability you dream about.

It may also help if you take the time to understand the workings of the human mind. Naturally, I can only share with you my understanding of these issues. You, are, of course free to pick and choose what to believe from the following. Much of this I learned from the experience of 40 years of dream interpretation, therapy and inter action with my Higher Self and Spirit Guides.
The mind or spirit is not physical like the brain. You existed as a sentient being before you were born and you will continue to exist after the death of your physical body. Five minutes after you are 'dead' you may feel nothing has changed. People who had a near death experience as a result of an accident or cardiac arrest often did not realize that they were 'dead' and seemed to return to their homes only to find that nobody could see, hear or talk to them. In a similar fashion, in the deeper levels of sleep, when we are not dreaming, the mind/spirit/consciousness can, in an exact replica of the physical body, travel to other dimensions and interact with other beings, living and 'dead'. Information and guidance can be gained in this way and become inter-woven into our

dreams.

The mind is divided into three parts – the conscious mind, the sub-conscious mind and the super-conscious mind. We function mainly in the conscious mind. This is the critical, logical, analytical and intellectual aspect. With this, we judge what is happening based on memories of similar situations and make decisions based on our intellect or emotions.

The sub-conscious is machine-like in the manner of a computer. It controls our emotions and the automatic functioning of the body. It was designed to function as a servo- mechanism and control the automatic functioning of the body such as breathing, heart rate, secretion of glands, immune system, creation and destruction of cells, etc. However, like computers it is only as good as it's programming. Negative belief systems and attitudes of our parents, siblings, teachers and other people who hurt us combined with memories from our birth, early childhood and former lives combine to help us to create a template or program in the computer – like subconscious which we call the 'self image'. This negative aspect of the sub-conscious is known as the Shadow Self. This can dominate and ruin our lives and health. It is not unlike an over-protective nanny which exceeds it's authority as a servant and limits the enjoyment and full potential of life. This will continue until, by a conscious and sustained effort of will power on our part we re-train or re- program it to work in our favor.

The super-conscious mind, also known as the Higher Self, Over Soul or conscience, is the 'spark of Divinity' that exists in all of us. It carries the memory of God from which it came and forever motivates us to return to the Source. We can do this with the inspiration it sends us in dreams to be involved in music, art, spiritual, philosophical activities. etc. It creates a new spiritual self image for us to show us how we can change and evolve into a better mind/spirit/consciousness. This is called the 'Real Self' and alignment with it can bring us closer to God. This harmony of body, mind and spirit is our Life Purpose.

FOREWORD

"THERE ARE MORE THINGS IN HEAVEN AND EARTH, HORATIO,

THAN ARE DREAMT OF IN YOUR PHILOSOPHY"

William Shakespeare

One night, I had a dream that so shocked me that I awoke in tears. I still remember the images in the dream; I was in a bathroom, there were cigarette burns on the ceiling, the roof was caving in and a friend, who was in my class at college at the time, was dead in the bath! The following morning, concerned for her wellbeing, I anxiously ran to find her and tell her my dream. As fate would have it, she happened to be working with George Rhatigan. She calmly assured me that she was not going to die and suggested that I write down the dream and send it to George. That was back in 2001. I wrote down the dream and received George's interpretation a few days later.

I learned that my dream was a warning showing me the negative consequences if I was to continue living as I was. George explained to me that my friend, dead in the bath, represented the loss of my own capacity to have children, my femininity. The cigarette burns on the ceiling, and the roof caving in, a potential nervous breakdown. It was a turning point in my life. Up until that time I had been experiencing digestive issues and occasional bouts of depression. I began to work with George to understand the root causes of my distress. I started a journey towards a greater awareness of the spiritual dimension of life and began a process of healing that has continued to this day. I have also witnessed the powerful effect that George's unique healing approach has had in the lives of others.

Every day, newspapers sell by the billions across the world. Collectively, we tune in to 'the news'. Radio news broadcasts are available on the hour every hour & newspapers proclaim the latest headlines: usually bad news. We hear about wars, violence, rape, climate emergency & natural disasters. In snappy headlines we absorb the sufferings of millions of people.

In a similar way, at night, we receive sophisticated

communication through our dreams. This is your own personal 'news' channel reporting on the one topic over which you do have control: You.

In the following pages you are about to learn how to understand, decode and also engage creatively and consciously with your dreams. Dreams are our own intimate and personal window to our lives and the world, at a deeper level. Rather than being passive consumers, our dreams offer us keys, tips, and an invitation to co-create our own lives and by extension, the world in which we live. While global news stations may inform our impotence, our dreams offer us a path to empowerment, insight, wisdom and inner spiritual growth and healing.

You may not remember your dreams. Perhaps there are some dreams that have been repeating for you. In the pages that follow, in George's wealth of knowledge and insight, you have at your disposal a powerful technology to re-wire your life from within.

In the Irish cultural tradition, we have "Aisling" poetry; powerful Vision Poems. In suffering oppression of language, culture and religion, material poverty meant that the Irish imagination has been developed to a great sophistication.

Dreams also invite us to dwell in hope and work through our imagination. In the Vision poetry tradition, a dream offers the solution, the remedy to the sufferings of both the poet and the people. It is through the dream that the spirit is kept alive. Our inner faculty of imagination, as Einstein once pointed out, is one of our superpowers as humans:

"Imagination is more important than knowledge. For knowledge is limited to all we now know and understand, while imagination embraces the entire world, and all there ever will be to know and understand." Albert Einstein

Working with the wisdom of your own inner teacher and spiritual guides through your dreams, you can access the powerful sub conscious mind. You will learn to understand the language of symbols, puns, images, colors and characters. As you engage through this world of vision and imagination, you open vast new possibilities for your life. Working on the inner canvas of dreams, navigating these inner realms, you can become a conscious ally in your own healing and begin to see improvements in every area of your life.

Television news broadcasts may get our attention, yet most of us tend to ignore or dismiss the inner news that is revealed in our dreams. The fate of life on the planet depends on our collective capacity for healing. Our survival calls us to use our power of Vision, Dream and Imagination. Rather than being passive victims, our dreams show us how we can become co-creators of Life.

One man's Dream inspired generations to hope, vision & courage when Martin Luther King proclaimed "I have a dream".

It is now time for all of us to reclaim the importance of our dreams, and begin to engage in healing our collective subconscious. It is my hope that you embrace the healing and soul-guidance offered to us in our dreams and become a co-creator with Life. Everyone has a role to play. George offers his vast experience, insights and guidance so that you too can access the power of your dreams. Let us dream a new dream for a bright new world.

Sharon Ní Chuilibín, 2022.

INTRODUCTION

WORKING WITH DREAMS

We all want to be healthy, happy, wealthy, 'lucky' and successful. Dreams indicate that these are our natural states of existence and anything less is an aberration. So, why are so many of us lacking in these areas? For these positive states to exist in our reality, they must first manifest in our consciousness. We create our own illness, depression, poverty, bad 'luck' and failure by the habitual way we think and feel about ourselves and other people. By the Law of Attraction, this pattern of negative thinking attracts deeper and deeper negativity, and we suffer as a result. In other words, we can bring bad luck on ourselves, exponentially, in a downward spiralling pattern.

Dreams are problem solvers. They indicate ways in which we can change our lives for the better by developing more positive thought patterns. Your issues and ailments are also caused by your bad habit of role playing. As a child you may have learned to get attention from adults by being ill or unhappy. But now, as an adult you may be still sub-consciously playing these roles. What can you expect to achieve but suffering and illness if you chose to be a victim? Dreams ask you to find and be your real self. By your "Real Self" I mean your future potential – including your ability to be happy, healthy, wealthy, lucky and successful. But to get there, you must first look at and accept your present time self with all it's faults and weaknesses. There is a saying; "To know one's self is the beginning of wisdom". When you plan a journey you must first decide where you are. It then becomes possible to see the way forward.

The 1st rule of life on this planet is to accept your body, including the male and female aspect, your physicality and spirituality, and all that involves. Whatever your difficulty, illness or issue might be in present time, it's origins can be traced back to how well you accept yourself.

Anything you think about deeply or concern yourself with during the day can become the subject of the nightly dramas in your sleep.

DREAMS ARE LIKE COMPUTERS

Like computers, they will:

(a) indicate the cause of your issue or ailment,

(b) suggest ways in which you can heal or improve it and

(c) invite you to participate in therapeutic dream activities – workshops in 'virtual reality' which can help you to face, confront and change the negative belief systems and fears which limit you from achieving your full potential.

You will find yourself engaging in strange and bewildering situations, meeting unusual people and animals, being exposed to strange colors, undergoing medical operations and procedures, crying, laughing, singing, running, jumping, falling, etc. etc. As strange as it may seem these adventures in what might seem like Alice's Wonderland are designed to heal and guide you in the pursuit of your goals and full potential.

Dreams will include healing, intuition, inspiration and encouragement into every aspect of your life including health, relationships, finance, spirituality and much more and all this will be done with great wisdom and insight. There is nothing new about this. Successful business people, inventors, artists, poets, scientists and authors have been taking advantage of this knowledge since the beginning of time. Many people, even those who do not remember their dreams find themselves waking up "feeling better" or knowing what to do about a problem. Such people would get even better healing and guidance if they learned how to fully read, understand and use their dreams.

To benefit from your dreams you may need to expand your mind to accept new ideas. You may need to, at least temporarily, allow for the possibility of there being a Higher Power sending you messages in your sleep. From the content of your dreams you will see that the sender is wise and intelligent. It is widely accepted that dreams are in a language or code, and common sense would indicate that you must already understand this cipher on some level of your consciousness. Otherwise there would be no point in sending it. Apply the techniques for decoding dreams in this book and understand how they can change your life for the better.

The extent to which you appreciate what the dream is trying to do for you in relation to some problem in your life and co-operate with the activities determines how much actual benefit and healing you receive. Dreams are designed to be inter- active. It can be like being on stage and having no script or understanding of the plot. Even though your body is asleep you still retain your free will. You can refuse, spoil, deny, avoid or run away from the drama. You also have the ability to change the scenery and characters by projecting your negativity onto people, objects, colours, etc. which were designed to heal and guide you. Naturally this can limit the benefits you experience.

So, what do dreams have to say about your problems? The message of dreams is very simple: If you want to change your life for the better, change your habitual patterns of thought, emotion and behaviour. This can make you feel better, less stressed and healthier. Your illness, your poverty, your unhappiness are simply bad habits which you may be able to change with the help of dreams.

These habitual ways of thinking and feeling about yourself, other people and the world in which you live are called your core beliefs – even though most of them have been passed down to you from your parents, family, ancestors, teachers, etc. Add to that, painful memories from your birth, early childhood and former lives and you end up with a collection of ideas, fears, and emotional reactions which you call your personality. The negative content of this will dominate your life and limit your health, happiness, wealth, 'luck' and success. This is called your Shadow Self and dreams will have much to say about how this sub-conscious part of you is responsible for the state you find yourself in, and the resistance you put up to the changes offered to you in dreams.

So, even with the resistance from your Shadow Self what can your dreams do for you in relation to your problems? To understand this see your dreams as a super-computer with access to past, present and future. Call it your dream machine. It is forever calculating and computing. In true computer fashion it can portray in imagery and symbols (it's own 'language') what damage you may be doing to yourself and asks "are you sure this is what you want? ". You are shown possible future scenarios – the worst case scenario if you persist with negative thinking and the best case if you opt for change. In the following chapters you will be shown how to re-enter your dream and communicate with the 'intelligence' that sent it to achieve your full potential.

HEALTH

Dreams are not medical diagnoses but they will focus on your most serious illness or the most threatening risk to your health. They will routinely show you the most likely emotional cause, present state of the problem and possible future outcome if circumstances remain the same. They may suggest changes in your lifestyle e.g. exercise, smoking, alcohol, diet, etc. In relation to the latter the focus is usually less about what you are eating and more about what is 'eating you'. In other words how repressed anger, guilt or grief can make you ill. You will learn and understand the effect of memories – especially from birth and early childhood on your health in present and future time. Who have you not forgiven in relation to perceived neglect, hurt or betrayal at your birth, childhood or in former lives? Dreams will bring you back to those times and ask you to re-evaluate, forgive and let go. Co-operating with this type of workshop can help you to understand illness on a deeper level. You can use this knowledge to help yourself and others.

RELATIONSHIPS

Most of us want to have happy personal relationships. We hope and expect the partner to 'make us happy'. If this does not happen we find someone else for the job. Eventually, we realize that we must first create the consciousness of happiness inside ourselves. Instead we may have been attracting partners into our lives who treat us in a manner we may not like but sub-consciously expect – usually based on the model we witnessed in our parents marriage. If your mother was abused, controlled, dependant, or whatever, are you experiencing something similar? We tend to get what we expect. Dreams will highlight the need to break out of this pattern and find a relationship which allows us to establish our real identity and find happiness in the process.

FINANCES, SUCCESS AND 'LUCK'

What belief systems do you sub-consciously hold about money, work, career, success, etc that keeps you in poor financial straits? Did you copy your father's work ethic? If he was unemployed or bad with money are you the same? Your dreams will leave you in no doubt as to the cause and remedy of your problem. You may believe that your success or failure is down to chance. Dreams indicate that we make our own 'luck' in what we bring on ourselves by the Law of Attraction. 'What you think is what you get'. If you think about being unemployed you get more of it. If you get a job, you are less likely to think in that fashion and more likely to get more job offers. Good 'luck', like health, wealth, happiness and success is our natural birth right. Our dreams are designed to bring these things to us. What you ask for may only come to you if you allow changes to happen in your life.

Everything has a vibration. If you can develop a state of openness and acceptance even if others around you are 'behaving badly' your vibration, ie. the message you project out into the universe, can be more positive and inviting. If it matches the vibration of what you desire, you can be more likely to get your wish. Re-entering and changing your dreams (as will be explained in the book) can also help in this regard. Moreover, opportunities for business or romance can depend on being in the right place at the right time. Understanding and working with your dreams can help you with this kind of synchronicity.

SPIRITUALITY

The human race is evolving whether consciously or sub-consciously and the motivation for this is coming to us in dreams. We are pre-programmed to be healthier, happier, wealthier, 'luckier' and more successful. But what else are we sub-consciously motivated to be, do or have? Each generation strives to be better than the previous one in terms of love, compassion, responsibility, etc. We are becoming kinder to the poor and disabled, more responsible for the planet, more inclined to freedom and democracy and so on. We are less tolerant of corruption, prejudice and hypocrisy. So, where are we going with this and where is it coming from?

You may not be interested in spirituality but spirituality is interested in you. Your soul, the spark of divinity in you which we call your Real Self, is the author and instigator of your dreams. This aspect of you is God-like and motivated by Love. It encourages you to be a better person and to use your God-given psychic and healing powers for your own benefit and that of others. You are expected to lose the negative traits and influences of your parents which were passed on to you and which now limit your spiritual progress. In this way you can align with your Real Self and take a step closer to God.

It should not seem strange to you to learn that before your soul entered the body you were pre-programmed in this way. This benevolence represents the perfect consciousness of your Real Self. This higher aspect of you is drawing you closer to itself. It asks you to be more like it in its perfection and to be motivated by love. This can help you to develop finer qualities like compassion, acceptance, tolerance, forgiveness, and so on. Before you came into the physical body you agreed as part of your Life Purpose to work on developing specific qualities that you lacked in former lives. You may now have consciously forgotten this commitment. Your dreams and this book will help you to remember precisely what you need to work on. Your soul or Real Self will also ask you to allow it to express itself in healing, psychic, spiritual, artistic or philosophical activity through you. You will be shown what spiritual gifts, powers and talents you possess. If you develop and use these abilities do not be surprised at the miraculous effects you can achieve. So, in addition to being healthy, happy, wealthy, 'lucky' and successful you are also pre-conditioned to be loving, healing and psychic. Compliance with all of this can bring peace, contentment and much more. Resistance, on the other hand can only mean unhappiness, illness and trouble. This not a threat or punishment – it simply means that if you go against your Real Self, and the Law of Attraction, the resultant mental conflict in the long term can lead to stress and physical ailments.

SOUL COMMUNICATION

Yes, communication and inter-action with your soul is possible and desirable. This can be done through re-entering a dream at any time after having it. This higher, wise and loving aspect of you is, after all the instigator of your dreams so what can be wrong with talking to the author? But what can you expect? It sent you into the Earth to occupy a physical body but it did not abandon you here. For eons of years and over countless lives it kept in touch with you in dreams- lovingly offering you healing, guidance and support. Now, you can reply to these communications on a conscious level-if you wish. To do so select a dream and using a short meditation you ask a series of questions. You 'listen' for the replies which will come telepathically. You will often be amazed at the wisdom and insight which will come to you on all aspects of your life. I have been doing this for over 40 years – over which time I have received enormous help and guidance. Much of the inspiration, information and techniques in this book have come to me from this source.

WELCOME TO

"HEALING WITH DREAMS"

1

WHAT ARE DREAMS, HOW DO THEY WORK?

The idea of a workshop i.e. learning by activity, seems to have originated in dreams. Practically every dream will invite you to engage in activities designed to heal and guide you in all aspects of your daily life. Your body is asleep and the rational, critical mind is 'on hold'. As a result, you cannot question why you are expected to fix the cooker, clean out the drains, drive a car without brakes or a steering wheel or other apparently pointless activities. It is only when you learn the symbolic meaning of the actions, objects, events, colors, etc. that you appreciate what the dream was trying to do for you. As in a code, everything in a dream can have a hidden meaning.

The cooker is often used to represent your digestion so the dream may be asking you to consent and co-operate while the dream heals this part of your functioning. The drains suggest your intestines which need cleansing. Driving a car without brakes and steering may be asking you to stop trying to control your life too much, and so on. Such dreams ask you for your consent and participation in the automatic healing and immune system of your body by reducing stress, going with the flow of life, being open to new ideas, and so on.

Even though you cannot rationalize what is going on in the nightly drama, you still retain your free will. You can refuse to co-operate with the activities, run away or otherwise spoil the efforts made by the dream to heal and guide you. If you do this, the dream is wasted and will be repeated another time using the same or similar symbols to get your consent and co-operation. The 'workshop' might include such activities as: walking, running, swimming = you need more exercise. The body is inclined to benefit from such exertions as it would in real life. "Shouting, screaming, crying" = You can safely release anger, fear and grief and de-stress your body in the process. If you agree to 'fix the clock, slates on the roof, a toilet bowl' or whatever, you send a message that you consent to the nocturnal healing of your heart "(ticker"), brain, elimination system and so on.

Dreams are like computers in that they invite you to interact with them. If you co-operate with the dream you can receive real physical, emotional and spiritual healing, guidance and inspiration. If you refuse, you must be prepared to accept some consequences. We all make these decisions every night and even though we forget most of it on awakening, some benefit will have got through. We may feel better or have some new idea or motivation. We rarely think about where it might have come from. How often have we gone to bed, troubled by a problem only to awaken with the solution? It is a good idea to write a question on a piece of paper, put it under your pillow and literally "sleep on it". The answer will invariably come in your dreams but you have to learn how to remember your dreams and to de-cipher them. That is what this book is all about.

"HOW DO DREAMS WORK?"

THE CHARACTERS

Every night an amazing theatrical drama is organized in which you (the dreamer) are an actor on stage.

You have no script and like Alice in Wonderland you must add lib and respond to what is happening however unusual or bizarre it might be. The actors are in three categories; Healing Agents, Guides and the Shadow Self.

HEALING AGENTS

Positive characters appear to encourage, support or heal you. Call these Healing Agents. They are mainly concerned with your physical, mental and emotional, health. The good personal qualities thy have or demonstrate such as acceptance, confidence, self-esteem, humor, love, etc are what you need to heal your body, avoid stress, illness, etc. This may relate to an ailment you have in present time or are likely to have in the future. You agreed, before you chose to reincarnate into this planet to develop these qualities as part of your Life Purpose. Healing Agents try to heal you by getting close to you in the hope that some of their positive qualities will "rub off" on you. They might get into bed with you or share a cup of tea and so on. Sometimes they want to touch you or perform unusual operations on your body such as "opening the upper part of the body" ("Open yourself to new ideas or emotions"). You have the ability to rebuff such overtures and strangely, you can change the character or appearance of these Healing Agents by transferring your inhibitions or fears onto them. For example, a very religious and inhibited lady who subconsciously believed that sex was evil dreamt that she was in bed with a male neighbor. In waking life she did not fancy him but in the dream he initially seemed attractive. In waking life she knew him to be sexually relaxed (the quality she needs). Everything seemed to be going well until she noticed that he had horns on his head and a tail. He was, "looking at her with an evil grin". She ran from the room.

This is typical of dreams in that the dreamer has the ability to alter the characters and scenery in accordance with his or her beliefs. We shall explore the subject of colours and their healing ability in later chapters but they too can be changed, darkened or 'polluted' with black (fear) if the dreamer wishes to avoid their effect. For example, in the sexual dream outlined above the color red might be used to arouse, impassion or stimulate the dreamer. She could change this into a mixture of red and black, maroon or limit it to stripes or borderlines – in line with her own repression. Similarly, green (the quality of emotional sharing) can be polluted or darkened to become 'bottle green' or 'combat green' to express her resistance to giving and receiving love.

GUIDES

Positive characters who have some authority, influence, a title or occupation such as kings, bartenders, taxi, bus, train drivers, etc. are what you may call Guides. They are mainly concerned with the spiritual development of the dreamer. Unlike the Healing Agents, the Guides are usually more remote, speak less and demonstrate by example what ability, talent, or gift the dreamer can develop or use. So for example, if you are consulting a healer or clairvoyant in your dream, then you have these abilities whether you know it or not. As with the good qualities of the Healing Agents you agreed to develop and use the gifts of the Guides as part of your Life Purpose. However, as when in the sexual dream the dreamer tried to avoid or limit the healing, you also have the ability to reject these spiritual or psychic gifts. In the dream they may turn out to be fraudulent – because this is what you expect. As is the case with Healing Agents, the Guides who enter the dream as, e.g. policemen, may become 'corrupt or drunken brutes', or whatever, in accordance with your prejudice. This is usually because your father may have had such failings or caused you to have them, and you expect the same from men – even in your dreams.

THE SHADOW SELF

Negative characters who appear usually reflect negative aspects of your personality or 'present time self'. You assumed this false persona mostly from memories of your parents. We call this your Shadow Self. Males appearing in your dream described as sick, angry, fearful, etc. indicate the negative effect that your father had on you while similarly limited female characters indicate the influence of your mother. If a negative character appears to be ill, then the type or position of such illness can indicate what you are doing to yourself because of the parent. For example if a male character has cancer of the colon, then think about what effect your father may be having on this part of your body. A sick female may indicate the effect of mum.

Everything, including people, children, animals, vehicles, appliances, etc. are divided into the same three roles.

Dreams are motivational workshops – theatrical psycho-dramas, if you will, to help you to get to know and accept yourself as a starting position from which to improve or develop. In waking life, the Shadow Self is an artificial creation incorporating the beliefs, fears and prejudices of your parents and negative memories from your birth, early childhood and former lives. It is a Frankenstein monster, made up of bits and pieces of other people haunting its creator. In real life, the Shadow Self is more like an overly protective nanny which hates any kind of change and limits your ability to enjoy life and take chances. It is driven by fear and obsessed with control. It curtails your ability to expand beyond the ideals, expectations and ambitions of your parents. In the process of exerting this control over your everyday life it can hinder your ability to achieve health, wealth, happiness, success and 'good luck' which is your natural state of being.

Your Real Self – as illustrated by the Healing Agents and Guides of your dreams, expresses the agenda of your soul or spirit. This part of you is the spark of divinity you inherited as a soul. It is wise and God-like, with insight into past, present and future. It carries the memory of God from which it came and will forever motivate you in dreams, art, spiritual, psychic, philosophical and artistic activities, and many other ways to return to the Source. It does not force you to obey. Instead it motivates you to return, time and again to reincarnate and learn to come in line with the idea of becoming a better person. If you look at your dreams as theatre, then the author of the 'plot' is your Real Self. It appears in the dreams as the authority figure and the Healing Agents. As the dream unfolds, you are expected to see the folly of not coming into line with the Higher Ideals indicated. It is an achievable ideal, and to the extent to which you consent and co-operate, you can be happier, healthier and achieve more of your potential in this life. The purpose of every life and every dream is to move you from the limitations of the Shadow Self and into the awareness of the Real Self. This usually puts you in conflict with the conditioning of your parents, teachers, culture, etc. which contributed to the creation of your Shadow Self. Dreams are all about the clash of these two ideologies. Learning to understand and work with dreams can raise your awareness and make it easier for you to bring your mind, body and spirit into alignment.

Fig.1. Guide, Shadow Self & Healing Agent

2

DREAMS AND THE LAW OF ATTRACTION

We often associate the word "Dream" with the idea of our 'heart's desire'. Everyday figures of speech like; looking for our "Dream Man" or as a put-down, when something seems impossible, we might be told: "*In your dreams!*" Yet, through working with our dreams and the Law of Attraction, what may have once appeared impossible can become possible.

Our dreams offer us unique insights, in symbolic form, into our attitudes, our beliefs, and how we perceive ourselves and the world around us. Our dreams also show us the condition of our health and potential health problems and how we may be blocking ourselves from achieving our "goals". The Law of Attraction operates on the basis that "like attracts like" – therefore, our dreams provide an early warning system of what we are attracting into our lives if the contents of our dream imagery should remain unchanged. If the message from your dream is a negative one, you must ask yourself – *"Is this what I want?"*. If there is a negative male or female character in your dream, nine times out of ten that is going to be dad or mum but also, because there's so many different dimensions to dreams, it can be others, it can be your partner, your husband or wife. Still, that doesn't cancel the negative male or female figure from being mum or dad on a different level. Ask yourself, *" What am I doing to myself, because of him / her?".*

One way to activate the Law of Attraction in our favour, is to learn to interact with our dreams. We can learn to re-enter our night dreams as we would a workshop, and interact and co-operate with the healing agents and our guides. with the contents of our dream to produce more positive results in waking life and experience. We have free will, even in our dream, we can choose to co-operate, or not.

But what is the Law of Attraction? The Universe is ruled and held together by natural laws such as gravity and the laws of physics. We cannot break these laws but we can offend against them which can bring about negative consequences. This should not be seen as judgement or punishment. It is simply cause and effect.

Our behaviour on the planet is governed by this Law of Cause and Effect which is otherwise known as Karma and Dharma, the Law of Attraction, or, Like attracts Like. What we send out to the Universe, even our thoughts, comes back to us in some shape or form sooner or later. The planet was designed to be a paradise as described in the Bible as the Garden of Eden. People were healthy and happy. They could have anything they wanted provided they lived in accordance with God's Laws. This still applies to us today. Knowing how to get want we want can help us to live in the natural way we were intended to be – i.e. happy, healthy, wealthy, lucky and successful but also loving, accepting, forgiving and of service to others.

For the Law of Attraction to work in our favour, we must be in alignment and in a state of acceptance. Moving – even a step closer to our Potential or Real Self (rather than the controlling 'nanny' like subconscious Shadow Self), can help to align us with the Law of Attraction. Our dreams can show us how we may be offending against this Law, and blocking ourselves perhaps by being too controlling, critical or judgemental in daily life. We are being asked to live from a place of Love and Acceptance. Developing such qualities and helping people by using our spiritual gifts and powers can be an integral part of our Life Purpose.

You may have a spiritual gift as a creative person and an ability to channel beautiful poetry or music. If you accept this gift of being a channel, you will be more in tune with your Real Self and closer to achieving your Life Purpose. Living in alignment with your Life Purpose means that the Law of Attraction can work for you. If you are out of alignment with your Real Self, you are out of alignment with the Law of Attraction. Your dreams will always indicate where you are in relation to this. Make a conscious effort to approach life with an attitude of Love and Acceptance rather than being judgemental and critical of yourself and others.

With practice, you can learn to decode your dreams and work with the Law of Attraction to activate your healing potential and attract luck and success into your life. Your dreams will indicate what spiritual gifts you may have or prompt you in some way to take a different view of life so as to fulfil your true potential. By using your gifts, you will be more likely to get what you desire in other areas of your life. For example, you may simply want money but your dreams may be telling you that to achieve this you may need to develop and use some latent ability or power. You may also have subconscious beliefs that contradict your conscious desires for health, wealth and success. These subconscious blocks will be revealed to you in your dreams. For example, you may feel that you do not deserve to be wealthy. If that is so, you may not experience abundance until you remove this subconscious belief system.

AN EXAMPLE

A businessman came to me. He had gone from being a millionaire to a bankrupt three times. The first time the tax man took his money. He then proceeded to gain wealth once again but the second time, his wife divorced him and he, once again became penniless. A third time, he generated millions only to lose it all once more with bad financial dealings. He came to me and said; "This could not be up to chance or luck – there must be something wrong".

THE DREAM

He gave me a dream where he had a huge amount of

stolen money hidden around the house. He was greatly stressed in the dream when two plain clothes police officers, a man and a woman, come knocking on his door.

This dream showed me that he had a conscious desire for money but a subconscious guilt – so any money that comes to him he will subconsciously reject. This subconscious guilt can also apply to the many people who win lotteries and lose it all.

I led this man back into his dream. The police officers were asked "What are you and what do you do?" They replied that they represented the Law (of Attraction). As detectives, their job was to expose hidden (sub-conscious) guilt and process it by Karma (illness, bad luck or loss) or Dharma (the female option of acceptance and service to others.). He had a choice to give himself up to one or the other. We discovered that he had a former incarnation in India in the 19thCentury when the British Army was there. He was in charge of a lot of treasure that the authorities had confiscated from a rich nobleman. He stole quite a bit of this and got away with it. His guilt from this past life was carried forward into present time. This is why he bankrupted himself. He believed that the only way he could forgive himself was to be of service. So, he opted for the path of Dharma. He went out to Africa and dug a well for a village to have water. That helped him to accept and forgive himself without any need for further stress, pain or loss. Dharma is another word for alignment with your Real Self and with making the Law of Attraction work for you. Karma is remaining with the Shadow Self and the Law of Attraction working against you.

The state of Acceptance is hugely important. It allows the Law of Attraction to work for you and good 'luck' to happen. It's all very well ordering things, but you have to allow it to happen. The State of Acceptance may be defined as;' If I can look at other people behaving badly in my opinion and feel no desire to change and control them I am in the State of Acceptance' This Law is not something you switch on or off. It is on all the time. You are e.g. either attracting poverty or illness or attracting luck and success. Your dreams will tell you whether it is working in your favour or against you.

With regard to money, vows of poverty from past lives can also get in the way of attracting money. Look out for nuns, monks or priests especially in appropriate places. A clear example of this would be to dream, as one man did, of a fat monk – like Friar Tuck from the Robin Hood story, stuck in the door of a bank and not allowing people to get their money in or out. You can see from this how a vow of poverty from a previous life can limit one's access to abundance.

LIKE ATTRACTS LIKE

Millionaires have been using the Law of Attraction for years. That is why a recent book on the subject was called 'The Secret'. It indicated how wealth (or a wealth consciousness) attracts wealth, while poverty (or a poverty consciousness) attracts more poverty. Rich people have been using this "secret" for hundreds of years. Now, it's time for the poor to think outside the box and choose to use the Law of Attraction to their own advantage.

In the same way that we create bad 'luck' and poverty with our negative belief systems, we can also bring chronic illness on ourselves. Like attracts like so, habitually thinking in a negative way attracts greater negativity. This can create a field of negative energy around you – preventing anything positive from coming your way. Moreover, this dark energy can become toxic and create serious illness in your body.

You may not understand the connection between your issue or illness, your dreams and the Law of Attraction. Rule no. 2 of Dream interpretation is all about Cause and Effect. It shows how everything that happens in your life has a cause – including your problems. Your dreams will show you how to use this knowledge to improve your life.

People can invoke the Law of Attraction without dreams but the advantage of dreams is that they will monitor your order and comment on your prospects of getting your wish. For example, you can use your computer to order anything you wish for when you are "online shopping". In a similar way, your dreams are tuned into the Law of Attraction. It would be pointless for Nature to give us a delivery system and no ordering mechanism. However, you must be clear about what you require. It can help enormously if you write out your "order" in your journal or diary. The subconscious will regard the written order as a contract. Simply thinking about what you desire and then changing your mind 10 minutes later can be a waste of time. You may, as some people do, place your written order inside this book, put it under your pillow and literally sleep on it.

Your dreams will immediately indicate how you may try to block or delay what you have asked to receive.

REFLECTIONS

It is important to consider whether your inner beliefs and attitudes are in fact blocking the prosperity, health and happiness that you naturally desire and is your birthright.

Consider the following:

- Are you too Critical or Judgemental about yourself or others?
- Are you Cynical about Life, Love or Happiness?
- Do you believe e.g. that money is *unspiritual* or "The Root of all Evil?"
- or that "Relationships can only bring Unhappiness",
- or, "I am a bad person and do not deserve Good Fortune" …?

For millennia, people have been seeking to invite the assistance of a higher power to ask for their heart's desire with prayer. Let us consider, what is prayer? Prayer is telepathic communication. Yet, who is going to hear the prayer and see that you get what you ask for? Basically, you are activating the Law of Attraction when you pray. With emotion and feeling you call for help, ask for what you need to God, Source, Creator, Higher Self, the Universe. Your spirit guides have a supportive role to play in all this. They will hear your prayer and use their access to a network of friends and helpers in the spirit world to deliver what you ask for. Whatever you want – they know someone who has it. That person will be prompted to go in your direction. But, as the saying goes, be careful what you pray for and how you go about doing it.

LOVE AT FIRST SIGHT

You may want a new relationship. You say or preferably write; "I choose to have a new relationship (supply exact details of what you want from the other person – personality, appearance, etc.) and in what time frame)-". What actually happens is that you will telepathically contact the person that you are destined to meet at deeper levels of sleep and agree to meet at a certain place and time over the coming days. When you wake up, you may have forgotten that such a telepathic meeting ever took place. The next morning, you may mysteriously have an intuition to go to a certain place.

You may not know why, but you feel that you are to go there. If you are a spontaneous person and you believe in your hunches and intuition, you may go. And so you will meet that person. You may think that it is "Love at first sight" but of course, it is not!

It may be that you will meet a potential partner that you are destined to meet or a potential business associate to help you with your work. When you meet the person, you'll have an instant reaction. This will be someone you have known over a number of lifetimes. This is how it is arranged. You are destined to meet them as you owe them some debt or you have unfinished business. You may have harmed them in another life and so you now have an opportunity to be of service to them or they to you, or both. The guides are working behind the scenes all the time. The other person will also be prompted. The success of your meeting depends on synchronicity: being in the right place at the right time.

Synchronicity provides a key indicator as to what extent we are in harmony with the Law of Attraction. We can cultivate a capacity to become more in tune with the subtle cues and intuitions from our dream life. People are being invited to develop their intuition and trust their gut feelings or “hunches”. It is important to use common sense as well. This is where the State of Acceptance comes in. When you develop this, you become more in tune with your intuition and more willing to go along with new ideas.

Dreaming of missing the train/bus or plane connection is one of the most common forms of dreams. I call it, “A funny thing happened on the way to the wedding”. In the dream, you are going to a wedding but you are in the wrong place, at the wrong time or not dressed properly for the occasion. That would indicate that you are missing opportunities. The same applies to business opportunities. You may want a partner but you may be sabotaging your chances by disturbing the network created by your guides and so you miss that key person you were meant to meet. Don’t worry. They will keep trying! But, what can you do to help the process? Look at your dreams. What are they telling you about the negative beliefs you may have about relationships, work issues, taking chances, etc, What is the pattern of your relationships? Is it a carbon copy of that of your parents? Perhaps you should think about ‘Cutting the Ties’ with their negative beliefs and traits.

Many of us struggle to trust our intuition yet through

re-entering and working with your dreams, you can develop this subtle guidance system within. Dreams will always try to bring you into balance and they don't allow you to be too extremist in one way or another. For example, if your energy is too male (logical, managing and controlling) you may be disregarding the importance of the female (sensitive, intuitive, emotional) aspect. Your dreams will always get you to strive to balance these different areas of yourself so that you can put new intuitive ideas to practical use.

"I CHOOSE"

When you work with the Law of Attraction it is important to consider your use of words. Your approach needs to be: "I choose to do, be or have …. " It is not effective to say "I want" or "I need" as these phrases suggest weakness. The subconscious mind responds better to commands, to authority and to confidence. This is why it is very useful to explore your own 'Control Dramas' and understand your personal communication style. You can learn more about the Control Dramas in Chapter 20 of this book.

Images, dramas, symbols and events that play out within our Dream life reflect the very real programming within our minds – our beliefs, our attitudes to health, money, relationships, success, even revealing spiritual gifts and abilities we ourselves may not be aware of. We can begin to take responsibility for these scenes of our dream life. As we learn to understand what they mean and how to change them around through re-entering our dreams, we can send a powerful message to our subconscious mind and begin to activate the Law of Attraction in our favour. Rather than being victims of our negative programming, we can choose to engage consciously and creatively in a process of re-wiring ourselves for success.

So you see, dreams are an important part of the mysterious missing link in the chain of cause and effect in the unfolding of reality. The Garden of Eden may seem like a fairytale but, the Law of Attraction still applies today as it did then. It may be hard to believe, but the planet is trying to move back to that state of Peace & Harmony. It is in all of our interests to embrace Dharma, through Love and Service, an attitude of Forgiveness and Acceptance. The capacity to shape our reality through the Law of Attraction is still there and can still work in our favour to create a more beautiful world through the power of our dreams.

3

FOUR RULES OF DREAM INTERPRETATION

S. C. A. R.

1.

Everything is me (SELF)

2.

Symbols are connected (CONNECTED)

3.

I try to avoid what I need (AVOID)

4.

I am responsible for events (RESPONSIBLE)

(S) SELF

Everything in the dream is a symbol representing an aspect of the dreamer. These are indicated by the four elements which make up life on the planet;

Earth –Air –Fire – Water

All the symbols are a variation of these.

EARTH

Solids such as a house, car, bicycle, the ground etc. = the physical body.

Any of the above described as damaged, defective, dried up, etc. = danger of physical illness. All the rooms in the building or the parts of the vehicle can represent different parts of your body. For example the stairs – a series of small platforms winding up inside the house = the spine. The toilet = elimination system, the kitchen = digestion and so on. Similarly, the roof of the car = the brain. Wheels = Circulation.

AIR

Wind, sky, interior of building, darkness, light = dreamer's state of mind

E.g. "thunderous winds", "heavy leaden sky" "untidy room" indicates how an angry, depressed or disordered state of mind can cause stress and trouble.

FIRE

Bombs, gunfire, volcanoes etc. = emotions, anger, fear, etc. Look for the potential consequences of your negative emotions e.g. dead bodies, derelict buildings, devastated land, etc.

WATER

Rivers, canals, lakes, etc. can refer to your spirituality, e.g. psychic / healing, art, culture, music, etc. The sea, rivers and rain can also life itself. For example "walking alongside a flowing river" =go with the flow of life, "Running in from the rain = fear of life, and so on.

Look for how the Shadow Self tries to limit your spiritual development and expression e.g, lakes (little or no outlet for expression), square pools, straight canals (man-made or artificial 'spirituality'), shallow water (limited understanding of spirituality). The state of water can also indicate blood issues.

(C) CONNECTED

All the symbols (places, people, children, animals, birds, fish, objects, colors, activities, puns, etc.) are linked to show you the cause and possible future emotional or physical effect of your present time mental state. Dreams are problem solvers, so whatever concerns you during the day will become the subject of your dreams at night. They will go on to indicate the cause of your problems or issues. People, e.g. appearing in the dream, apparently standing by as chaos or damage occurs can have a bearing on the problem. In other words, correlation = causation. For example; a man had a dream which took place at work. His boss (male) was criticizing his work while a nearby central heating radiator bursts. (The central heating refers to the circulatory system of the body). Most likely the stress of trying to live up to his father's impossibly high standards was affecting his blood pressure. Dreams offer healing and guidance on whatever concerns you. You usually wake up with the solution in your head –

whether you remember the dream or not. Here is another example; A woman dreamt that she was in the kitchen mixing ingredients in a bowl. ('Bowl' is a pun for 'bowel). A female neighbor was present. The dreamer became so upset that she damaged the bowl. (Stress from memories of her mother is affecting her digestion and elimination). The male and female characters in the above dreams seem incidental to the damage to the physical objects (dreamer's body) but they represent the parents and are the cause of the problem.

This Rule highlights the connection between dreams and the Law of Attraction (also known as the Law of Cause & Effect). It shows how, everything we think, feel and do in relation to ourselves and others can effect us in present or future time. So, don't think badly about yourself or anyone else for more than 60 seconds. After that time, by this Law, you can attract negative energy, illness, bad "luck" and trouble to yourself.

The rule can also be applied when a positive character appears in a dream indicating repairs, improvements, good 'luck' etc.

(A) AVOIDANCE

What the dreamer tries to avoid, deny, limit or run from in the dream is what he or she needs in waking life. For example; how often have you run away from someone who tried to heal or get close to you in a dream (Healing Agent)?

(R) RESPONSIBILITY

The dreamer is always responsible for what happens, has happened or may happen in the future. This indicates how the Shadow Self can sabotage the dreamer's plans or ambitions unless it is re-trained to do otherwise. Look out for delays at airports, bus stops, (missing opportunities or putting off new enterprises), trouble on the way to a wedding (avoiding meeting prospective partner or dreamer's issues with relationships.) This Rule asks us to take Responsibility for what we bring on ourselves by the Law of Attraction.

4

UNDERSTANDING YOUR DREAMS

Basically, all dreams are workshops dealing with your issues and ailments. Invariably, they contain (a) healing from the Healing Agents (b) guidance from your Guides and (c) objections from the Shadow Self in relation to the subject matter. The latter, most likely will be indicated by the location. This is the most important symbol because in addition to giving you the subject matter it may also indicate your state of mind (cause of the problem). So, if your dream has you in hospital then it will usually go on to indicate how your state of mind can make you ill. If you are in a location with a partner or prospective lover then the subject matter can be relationships and how your state of mind can limit them. The usual pattern is as follows:

(a) You find yourself in a healing scenario. A positive person (Healing Agent) is on the scene. You may know this person in waking life as e.g. a kindly and sympathetic woman. If she is a stranger to you she may demonstrate such feelings. A doctor is attempting to give you or some other person some form of healing or therapy. (Healing Agents may appear in any shape or form such as positive people, animals, fish, birds, etc. or inanimate objects.) If, e.g. a bicycle or track suit is there then exercise may be needed to improve the situation. You may be invited to take part in some kind of activity and so on. (Every dream contains at least one healing device and usually many more. The symbolic significance of everything positive should be considered.). Such dreams, unless you are working on yourself and developing your awareness end with you rejecting or sabotaging the healing.

(b)You find yourself in a spiritual setting. Guides appear and demonstrate some gift or power. You reject it and so on.

EXAMPLES:

(A) HEALING

The Law of Attraction (Cause and Effect) rules all

aspects of Life on the planet, including health issues. Dreams help you to see the connection between habitual negative thinking and emotion (the cause) and chronic illness (the effect). For example, let's say the setting is a hospital. (A hospital or therapy centre usually can indicate the effect the dreamer's personality or state of consciousness can have on his health.) You are looking at an angry man in a bed. His skin is covered with blisters. (Applying Rule 2 "Connectedness" you link the anger with the condition and conclude that anger associated with his (your) father has 'boiled his (your) blood' and created the problem) A relaxed young woman wearing tan colored clothes sits at his bedside (Healing Agent – the color tan indicates acceptance – the quality you, the dreamer need to heal or avoid this illness). A doctor appears (Guide / Healing Agent) and attempts to touch the patient with his hand, (Indicating that the dreamer has" hands – on healing" ability.) You, or the person being treated reject the healing – leave or simply watch as the appearance of the scenario or those present 'darken' or negatively change.

(B) GUIDANCE

The guidance you receive in dreams is often in

relation to your spiritual gifts and powers. Developing and sharing these with others can align you with your Real Self, and by the Law of Attraction, bring down healing energy on yourself. The location of Dreams generally indicates the subject matter and because these gifts and powers are your most valuable asset such dreams will often involve valuable items of jewellery. For example, gold and silver.

Example of such dreams include visiting a jewellery shop. You enter a jewellery shop to buy a gold ring (Gold is associated with the energizing effect of the sun and indicates energy healing.) The shop assistant (Guide) offers you a silver necklace (Silver is linked to the light or enlightenment of the moon and indicates intuition or clairvoyance. The necklace is the expression of such a gift). You refuse the offer and leave the shop.

All too often, we reject our spiritual gifts. This can cause conflict. This mental conflict can result in physical ailments. Denying your clairvoyance, for example, can result in eyesight issues. Not listening to your guides or rejecting the words you hear from them can cause tinnitus or deafness.

THE 'IRMA DREAM'

Doctor Sigmund Freud was known as the "father of psychoanalysis" and a pioneer in the field of dream interpretation. The following is a dream he had about Irma a patient he was treating for hysteria in 1895. I find it a good idea to give dreams a title. I call this dream "Open Up". In the light of what you have read so far have a go at interpreting it. – The dream takes place in a large hall where he is entertaining other doctors. Irma arrives. She is suffering dreadful pains especially in her throat. He was angry with her and said "It's your fault". Then he became concerned and somewhat guilty – in case he had missed something in his diagnosis of her condition. He tried to look into her mouth but she had great difficulty trying to open it. He took her to a window to get a clearer vision. She eventually opened up and he could see inside. She had "a large white patch and extensive whitish-grey scabs on the right hand side. Doctor M, a colleague, was there and "strangely clean shaven" instead of with his usual beard. He gave a positive prognosis when asked for a second opinion. Another doctor gave her an injection of chemicals – presumably in the mouth "possibly with a dirty syringe"

INTERPRETATION

Read again the Four Rules of dream interpretation and apply them to the dream. List the symbols as 'positive' and 'negative'. Who is playing the roles of the Shadow Self, Guide or Healing agent? What healing devices and activities are used and why?

Working on the dream led Freud to invent psychoanalyses. In his book 'The Interpretation of Dreams' he admits that he had 'no notion of what it meant."

However, because he was so obsessed that illness was caused by repressed sexuality the part where the doctor injected Irma in the mouth with a syringe suggested to some experts that sex would be the cure for her illness. Freud was so pleased with his findings that he wanted a plaque put up on the house where he 'interpreted' the dream. Sadly, twenty eight years after the dream he died of cancer in the same part of his mouth as indicated by the dream.

Ten people can look at a dream and come up with as many different interpretations. So, does that mean that only one is correct and nine are wrong? Not, necessarily. All can be valid because dreams can be interpreted on many different levels by looking at the same symbols in different ways. This is because dreams are infinite and can heal and guide the dreamer on various levels or dimensions. These can include glimpses of the past (birth, early childhood, former lives), possible future events, the cause and possible effect of memories on present or future time, sex, health warnings and much more. I offer my understanding of the dream without suggesting that it is the only one.

MY INTERPRETATION

I interpret dreams by listing negative symbols under "I am" and positive symbols under "I need". Positive symbols suggesting talent, power or potential can go under "I can be". All of the above are then applied to what I believe to be the subject matter which can be determined by the location. The dream takes place in a large hall where Freud was entertaining other doctors so he is asked to extend and broaden his state of mind in relation to health and the treatment of illness. (He is entertaining other doctors so the dream asks him to entertain new ideas in relation to health/healing (young men symbolize new ideas – young women =emotional change), Irma plays the role of Freud's mother and what he is doing to himself because of her i.e. sub-consciously creating illness in himself.(Remember Rule 1: 'Everything in your dream is an aspect of yourself' – so Irma is an aspect of his Shadow Self) The healing devices include (1) "opening of the mouth" = "express how you feel" (2)"moving into the light of the window"="use intuition or enlightenment", (3) "looking into Irma's mouth"= "look into yourself." (4) Doctor M. is also a Healing Agent in that he has a positive future outlook and appears having shaved off his beard (removed facial growth – symbolic of eliminating facial cancer) is barefaced or open about facing issues. (5) the various other doctors – suggesting a diversity of alternative medical techniques (6) The doctor injecting Irma would have a placebo effect on Freud's subconscious mind. However, the fact that it then turns out to be done with "a possible dirty syringe" would suggest an element of avoidance or self sabotage. (Rule 3) (7) Freud himself is also a Healing Agent because he is trying to heal himself by treating Irma.

Freud believed that sexual repression can create illness and his followers would point to the obvious sexual implication of the syringe being put into Irma's mouth and this may be a valid viewpoint. But, the suggestion that the syringe is dirty would indicate that he may have sub-consciously believed that sex was dirty. Other experts who looked at this dream suggest that the syringe may indicate Freud's chain smoking of cigars and the danger this posed to his health.

Most dreams have a re-birthing dimension so his repressed feelings probably have their origin at his birth. See the large hall as the womb. Freud is comfortable here until the front door opens and Irma appears. She is in great pain and expecting him to help her. He reacts by feeling angry, concerned and guilty. This is how he felt at his birth but he could never openly express thesesentiments. The repressed feelings created negative energy in the mouth area which eventually became toxic and cancerous. The colors of the cancer –white and whitish-grey are significant. White in dreams indicates a judgmental perfectionist attitude while grey is the denial of emotion – so is he denying or bottling up his judgment of his mother? Guilt at the pain he caused to her by being born may have motivated him to become a doctor. This is typical of the re-birthing aspect of dreams which usually indicate the effect of birth on the personality and health of the dreamer in present and future time.

Was the cancer inevitable? Not necessarily. The

purpose of such health warnings in dreams is to motivate the dreamer to avoid a negative outcome or at least learn from it. Dreams, like computers can indicate the most likely future outcome of a set of circumstances in past or present time. In this case refusing to express how he feels about his mother creates toxic energy in his mouth which eventually becomes cancerous. This is a calculation rather than a prophesy. In negative dreams you are informed of what you are doing to yourself and then asked: "are you sure this is what you want"? Again, like a computer the dream invites you to interact with it and reply. If you do so there can be a different outcome. This can be done by a brief meditation, re-entering and changing the dream. This sends a message to the sub-conscious mind that you want a different outcome. Edgar Cayce had a saying; "A dream not interpreted is like a letter unread". My attitude is; "A dream not re-entered and changed is like a letter unanswered." I shall explain this in greater detail shortly.

5

TECHNIQUES FOR DREAM INTERPRETATION

METHOD A:

"I AM. I NEED. I CAN BE"

(1) Write your dream out in as much detail as possible. Leave a margin to the left and right hand side of the page. Over the left margin write: "I am" and "I need" over the right. Make room at the top for a title and at the bottom for the words "I can be".

(2) Read the dream a number of times and using different colored pens underline positive and negative words and phrases. List all the negatives

under "I am" and the positives under "I need". If you are not sure whether a word or phrase is positive or negative list it under both. Any positive word or phrase that suggests a talent, ability or power list it under; "I can be." This can include electrically powered appliances such as radios, television sets, powerful cars, and spiritual gifts such as, healing or psychic ability, etc.

(3) Consider the location with regard to what might be the subject matter of the dream and give it a title. For example, if the location is a hospital then the subject matter will usually be your health and (as in the case with Freud's dream) what factors can influence it – negative memories, beliefs, emotions, diet, lifestyle, etc. A dream involving interaction with a member of the opposite sex might be about relationships. A bedroom scene could suggest sex and so on. A dream about work usually means working on yourself. If the location changes – say from the bedroom to the kitchen then it might be a different dream. Give the dream a title which you think sums up its essence.

(4) When you have decided on the subject matter then all the characters and activities must have some bearing on it – in short to heal, guide or object. The

positive Healing Agents and Guides (your Real Self) will try to give you healing and guidance. The negative characters (your Shadow Self), unless you have been working on yourself and re-training this part of your mind will do their utmost to spoil, limit or sabotage the effort. They can do this by denial, avoidance or changing the scenery, characters, and colors in accordance with your negative conditioning. Sometimes you are an onlooker to this conflict or at other times you may play the role of the Shadow Self. If you have been working on yourself and have developed some level of awareness you may find yourself acting as the Guide or Healing Agent, as in Freud's dream in which he was trying to heal himself.

EXAMPLE

HEALTH, WORK, SPIRITUALITY AND BIRTH

"I was driving my car along the North Circular Road. I was late for a business meeting and getting stressed by the traffic and the bad state of the road. I noticed a young man at the side of the road dressed in a dark green track suit and trainers. He looked in a bad way. I offered him a lift. He accepted and got in. We continued on our way. Then the engine of the car seemed to be under pressure. I stopped at a garage. The mechanic there wanted to sell me a high –powered Mercedes. I told him I could not afford it."

The road system in a dream (especially circular, main or arterial roads), usually refers to the circulatory system so the subject matter is his heart and circulation. Look at this dream as healing and guidance on his health, birth, spirituality and work. So when it comes to these issues:

I am – "late, stressed, bad state, dark green, in a bad way, under pressure"

I need -"track suit and trainers, garage"

I can be – "mechanic, high-powered Mercedes"

Is the dream any clearer now? Dreams do not simply tell you that you have or had a particular problem with your health, work, spirituality or birth. They more often indicate the cause and how you can deal with it. They then set about healing the issue. This is where Rule 2 comes in. Look at the dream and connect apparently unconnected symbols to show cause and effect.

MY INTERPRETATION

In dreams the physical body is normally indicated

as a building or vehicle, car, bus, etc. – the state of which can suggest possible physical illness in present or future time. So when you look at this man's dream it is obvious that his heart (engine) and circulatory system (North Circular Road) need attention. Blood pressure perhaps. Green is a healing color for the heart although here it seems darkened by fear (black) or anxiety. So he needs to get checked out by a doctor (mechanic).

When you look at the dream from the birth aspect then the building or vehicle can represent mother's body at, before or soon after the birth. This is where all his problems are coming from. The car (Mum) is "under pressure" suggesting that his mother was unwell at his birth. The young man (the dreamer as a baby) is outside the car- meaning he has just been born and is in a" bay way". The dreamer plays the role of the Healing Agent and offers him a lift. This refers to the first meeting of the child with his father. If Dad had physically picked him up – that simple gesture would have boosted his confidence and helped him to be more at home on the planet. Male Healing Agents try to make up for what qualities the dreamer's father lacked – in this case being supportive.

Because of the circumstances of his birth he is less grounded and calm especially in the workplace. Every day is stressful ("stressed with "traffic"- meaning business").It has caused him to have a poor sense of time and place ("late for business meeting") So he is not inclined to be in the right place at the right time and as a result misses opportunities.

From a spiritual viewpoint the powerful car means he has healing abilities but lacks the commitment to develop it. ("Cannot afford it").

Fig.2 : The Magic Mirror of Dreams

6

TECHNIQUES FOR DREAM INTERPRETATION

METHOD B:

RE- ENTERING DREAMS

Dreams are inspirational messages going from your soul to your sub-conscious mind in a symbolic language that is understood by that part of your consciousness. So, you know, on some level of your awareness what the message means – otherwise why send it? The conscious, logical, critical part of your mind might not be able to make any sense of it because the message is not meant for that part. So, sometimes it is necessary to by-pass the conscious mind, access the sub-conscious and ask it to interpret the dream – not unlike gaining entry to the memory banks of a computer, The content of the transmission is always of a high moral standard but because of the avoidance (Rule 3) tactics of the Shadow Self there may be some negative input and distortion.

In a nutshell, nobody knows better than the dreamer what the dream means. The problem is that dreamers do not know that they know. This is why a short meditation is needed to bring about a relaxed mental state to by-pass the sensor of the conscious mind and open the door to the sub-conscious. When access is gained the dreamer will find himself interpreting it – often with remarkable insight and wisdom. However, he or she must be prepared to express spontaneously what comes to mind.

Procedure: Read the dream a number of times and memorize it. Isolate the positive symbols from the negative. Take note of anything that stands out as inappropriate to the circumstances e.g. "a bull in a china shop", "an elephant in the room", "a nun in the bedroom" and so on. Call this the focal or talking point. The idea is to address some of these symbols – especially the focal point and the location – as if you have just arrived from Mars and don't know what e.g. a bed, bus or taxi is or does. This enables you to understand the symbolic meaning of these symbols. It can be a good idea to start with an inanimate object. The critical, analytical part of the brain cannot deal with this idea so the intuition takes over. For example "What are you?" – Answer; "I'm a bed". "What do you do?"Answer; "I provide facilities for rest, sleep and sexual expression"

Example: A woman had a dream in which she was in bed with a man. A nun came out of a closet. There was an Alsatian dog in a cage in the corner of the bedroom. I shall use this dream to illustrate the procedure.

THE 4 MINUTE MEDITATION

(1) Sit or lie down in a comfortable position at a time and place in which you are unlikely to be disturbed. Have someone read the following mediation or play it back to yourself on a recording.

(a) "Take a deep breath and just when you think your lungs are filled with air draw in more. Hold it as I (slowly) count to 4 – 1 2 3 4

Now slowly exhale to the count of 4 – 1 2 3 4 and

release all the tension in the lower part of your body from your thighs to your toes. (Pause)

(b) Breathe in deeply again. Hold it for the count of 4 -1 2 3 4. Now slowly exhale to the count of 4 – 1 2 3 4 – releasing all the tension and stress from the centre of your body – your stomach and intestines (Pause)

(c) Breathe in deeply again. Hold it for the count of 4– 1 2 3 4. Now, slowly exhale to the count of 4 – 1 2 3 4 and release all the tension and stress in the upper body – chest, shoulders, neck, lungs, heart and spine (Pause)

(d) Breathe in deeply again. Hold it for the count 4- 1 2 3 4. Now, slowly exhale to the count of 4 – 1 2 3 4 and release all tension and stress from your head and brain" (Pause)

"You now find yourself in an open field. Up ahead you can see a set of steps. There are 10 steps down. In a moment I will slowly count down from 10 to 1. With each count you will relax deeper and deeper. At the count of 1 you will be in a deep state of consciousness in which anything is possible. 10....9...8.......relaxing deeper 7....6....5...deeper and deeper.... 4...3...2...1....You now back in your dream. Your attention is drawn to one of the symbols."

UNDERSTANDING THE DREAM

Returning to our example:

A woman had a dream in which she was in bed with a man. A nun came out of a closet. There was an Alsatian dog in a cage in the corner of the bedroom.

Re-entering the Dream:

(1) *"What are you?"*

(Answer) I'm a nun in a bedroom?"

(2) *"What do you do?"*

(Answer) "I abstain from sex in accordance with my vows of chastity, poverty and obedience from a former life as a nun".

(3) *"What aspect of me or my life do you represent ?"*

(Answer) "The guilt I feel when the subject of sex, money or disobedience is raised". (Because the scenario is negative the following question is then asked):

(4)*"What am I doing to myself because of you?"*

(Answer) "I'm limiting my ability to enjoy, sex, money and freedom"

(If there is what appears to be a positive symbol present e.g. a man in the bed, then you talk to him.)

"What are you?"

(Answer) "I'm a man in the bed."

"What do you do"

(Answer) " I get close and intimate".

(5) *"Why do I need you in my life at this time?"*

(Answer) "I provide, sex, support, comfort, etc". (Here the dream can provide clarity about what you want and need from a relationship).

THE SIX QUESTIONS

The six questions are always asked in this order:

(1) What are you?

(2) What do you do?

(3) What aspect of me (or you if you are doing this to another) or my life do you represent?

At this point you have a choice. If the scenario is negative you ask:

(4)"What am I doing to myself (my life, health, relationships, etc.) because of you? If the scenario is positive ask;

(5) "Why do I need you in my life at this time?

The final question can be:

(6) How can I change this dream so that I can get the full benefit of the healing and guidance and send a positive message to my sub-conscious mind, the Universe, Powers that be, or whatever?

Important:

When the procedure is over count the dreamer back by saying:

"In a moment I will count from 1 to 5. As I count feel yourself coming out of the meditation. (1) Waking up now (2) more awake (3) all the feeling coming back into your body (4) fully awake now (5) fully awake, feeling very positive and confident."

When the above questions were applied to the other symbols it became clear that the dreamer was inhibited (the closet), caging or repressing her natural (animal) sex instinct and love (the dog) and so on. When asked how to change it around she chose to remove the limiting symbols – nun, cage, closet and inter- act with the man in the bed. Repeating this over a period of time can re-train her sub-conscious Shadow Self to be less inhibiting. In this way she can improve her sexual response, attract and retain more money and be more open to change.

When you are using this method to help other people interpret their dreams, begin by putting them into the relaxed, altered mental state. Encourage them to select a symbol. Start with the focal point of the dream and then go on to deal with some of the others. Next, ask the six questions in the sequence shown. They must answer quickly and spontaneously. This technique is far superior to the "I am. I need, I can be" one described in the previous chapter because it by-passes the intellect and contacts the Real Self. This is the 'golden door' to communication with the soul. The knowledge and wisdom that will flow from ordinary people using this technique will sometimes astound you. In this way you can develop your channeling skills and that of others. Your own Real Self will help you to interpret the dreams of other people even if they are not present when you do so. Naturally, you should ask for their permission.

7

HEAL YOURSELF BY CHANGING YOUR DREAMS

When you have re-entered your dream and communicated with the characters you find that the dream has explained itself. What was conveyed in obscure symbols is now expressed telepathically in plain language. But, remember you were only able to do this by putting yourself into an altered state of mind. You did this by using, perhaps, the 4 minute meditation as explained in the previous chapter. In this state of consciousness you will know intuitively how the dream should be changed so that you can get the full benefit of its healing and guidance. Doing this on a regular bases can be of enormous benefit for two reasons:

(a) you can re-train or re-program the computer-like Shadow Self to react differently to certain situations involving e.g. people, animals, alcohol, cigarettes, food etc. etc. and

(b) you can develop your psychic and healing abilities.

Armed which the knowledge of how you avoided, denied, changed or ran away from the healing and guidance in the original version of your dream, you can now intend to inter-act differently with the Guides, Healing Agents and aspects of the Shadow Self.

THE GUIDES

The authority figures in your dreams attach great importance to your spiritual gifts, powers and talents which they usually demonstrate by their occupation or title. Developing these abilities and specific good qualities can be essential aspects of your Life Purpose and activate the Law of Attraction in your favour. When they were offered to you in the dream, you may have denied or avoided them. For example, a lady had this dream "I was bringing a gift to Princess Anne. The gift cost £200 but I managed to get it for £48". She knew that the dream was about accepting her spiritual gift but she did not know what that ability or talent was. When she re-entered and asked Princess Anne; "What do you do?" the answer was, "I stand in for the queen". 'Stand-ins', agents, postal workers, actors, singers musicians, etc. are all middlemen, in that they either act for higher authority or convey something written by one party and bring it to another. So she realized that her gift was channeling and she was undervaluing it. She asked the princess how to change the dream around which she did.

If there is no authority figure in your dream you can bring one in and take guidance from him or her as to how to alter the dream. He or she might tell you to take the gift – the gold (healing,) the silver (intuition), the pearls, (wisdom) and so on. You might be told to "talk" to deceased relatives or friends (channeling) and so on. This communication with the Guide, a discarnate soul who is wise and knowledgeable can be a new and exciting experience. It is not unlike feeling that you have discovered treasure in your attic. Developing and using these powers can work wonders for your self-esteem. You can learn a lot about yourself, the world and other dimensions. This was how I came to write this book.

HEALING AGENTS

The Healing Agents in your dreams will usually set out to heal you in various ways. You may know them in waking life to be confident patient, compassionate or whatever or they demonstrate such qualities in the dream. By implication they suggest that by developing these qualities in yourself you can avoid or heal the issue, illness or problem. Simply ask the Healing Agent the question; "Why do I need you in my life at this time?" All will be revealed to you. You may be told to repair damaged parts of the house, car or bicycle, (physical healing), cleanse and re-decorate a bedroom your dream described as "narrow and filthy" (psychological healing of the belief that sex is dirty) and so on. In the altered state wonderful new healing techniques will be applied and as in the case of the Guides if no Healing Agent is present you can bring one in.

SHADOW SELF

This is the spoiler, the one who puts a limit to your potential and enjoyment. Remember, it is driven by fear and obsessed with control. In dealing with this aspect of yourself three words come to mind – 'confront, communicate and change'. The Guide and Healing Agent suggest new techniques in order to improve your issue, ailment or problem. The Shadow Self fears any kind of change and now it gets an opportunity to express its objections to the healing and guidance. So when you confront a man from your dream who was described as e.g. "intimidating, weak, ill," or whatever the key question will be: "What am I doing to myself because of you?"

Most likely, this will be the 'shadow' of your father. So, have you copied him and become a bully or gone the opposite way and are now timid? Have you 'picked up' his illness? Next communicate with him in a way that perhaps you never could in waking life. Why did he act the way he did? The answers will come intuitively. Finally act as if you accept, forgive and release him (and yourself) from the limitations of the relationship. The dream in which this negative character appears might mention parts of a house or car and even suggest damage there e.g. the plumbing (liver or kidneys) or the wheels (circulatory system). These can indicate the physical effect that a negative aspect of your father had and has on your body (Rule 2). You may need to call in workers or experts to repair, re-furnish or re-decorate.

Focus on what aspects of your functioning the dream indicates that you have difficulty accepting. This non-acceptance can energetically starve some organ, gland or system or create negative energy there. The result can be real physical illness. Remember the 1st Rule of life – accept your body. When you re-enter the dream indicate your acceptance of this aspect of yourself. For example if you do not accept your sexuality the reproductive system can suffer, If you do not accept emotions the heart can fail and so on. Rule 3 of Dream Interpretation – what you try to avoid is what you need (to accept), can help you here.

8

ASPECTS OF DREAMS, DREAMING AND LIFE

What do dreams say about your health, career, relationships and spirituality? For thousands of years, people of all creeds and cultures including the Egyptians, the Greeks, the Romans, the Chinese and many others believed that dreams were important and came from God. Even in the words of the ultra -conservative Roman Catholic Church: "Somnia a Deo missa" (*Some dreams are sent by God*), we find an acceptance of their spiritual dimension. But why were so many of these ancient people convinced of this? Is there a consensus of belief among scholars today as to what dreams are? Are they, as many people believe coded messages traveling from one part of the mind to another? Do they contain information consciously unknown to the recipient, insight into the future, a deeper understanding of the cause and solution of our problems, issues and illnesses? In my original profession as a police officer I was always interested in investigating and solving mysteries by getting to the truth. For that reason dreams fascinated me. I found that trying to make sense of them intellectually was almost a waste of time. Dream dictionaries were also no help to me. To understand them I needed to mentally 'travel' to the dimension from which they came. I needed to communicate with their author. I did this by devising a quick system of meditation and re-entering old dreams.

Using this meditation I found myself telepathically communicating with a wise and intelligent source. Some of this came from advanced spirits we call Spirit Guides and other parts came from my soul or Real Self. This latter aspect of myself sent me the dreams and invited me to participate in their activities. In this way my questions about dreams, life, death and the hereafter were answered. I asked it to help me formulate a system of interpretation, which for the first time in history could enable the ordinary 'man in the street' to understand dreams and use their wisdom to heal himself and others. The result can be found in the following pages.

Interpreting a dream is easy. The difficult part is making sense of the interpretation. This is because dreams deal with ideas and concepts that are unfamiliar to most people such as Re-incarnation, the Spiritual Laws of Attraction, Karma and Dharma, Spiritual Gifts, Life Purpose, Spirit Guides, Shadow Self, Male and Female Aspects and so on. As any code breaker can tell you – knowing what to expect from the encrypted message can make it easier to understand.

(A) THE 'VOICE' WITHIN

If you could talk to God what would you ask and what would you be told about your health, relationships, choice of work, spirituality or lifestyle? You may not be able to talk directly to the Creator but you can learn how to communicate with your soul – the God aspect – the spark of divinity inside yourself – that part of you that is God. What I learned from these meditations is that this aspect of you sent you to Earth as a spirit to occupy a human body. It did not abandon you here and never lost contact with you. It heals and guides you in your dreams and arranges for Guides (guardian angels) and friends in Spirit to assist you on your journey through life. It knows your past, present and possible future. It sends you messages every night, comments on your thoughts', ideas and activities of the day and prepares you for upcoming events. It 'scans' your body looking for possible health issues and devises dream scenarios to heal what weaknesses it finds. The dreams it sends are in the form of theatrical drama or workshops in which you are expected to play your part – even if you do not know or understand the plot. This spiritual aspect of you, as I shall explain in greater detail later will appear in these nightly dramas as the authority figures – doctors, nurses, police officers, etc who indicate – usually by example what is required from you. It has prepared healing activities in which you are invited to take part. You are expected to interact with the other actors in order to receive healing and guidance in various forms. However, you retain your free will – even in a dream and you can work with the dream or against it. The extent to which you co-operate determines the amount of benefit you receive. When you wake up you usually forget the entire experience but at least some of the healing and guidance remains.

(B) YOU CHOSE TO BE YOU

Many of your dreams will help you to understand difficulties you may have with family relationships. You did not drop randomly into your parent's family. In the Spirit World before you were born you chose your physical body, your parents, your country, the 20th or 21st century, etc. for a reason. Moreover, you were or are destined to meet people who will become your husband, wife, partner, offspring, etc. Most likely you knew them in former lives. You may have unfinished business with them. Meeting with them again is not a matter of luck. It is all carefully arranged and synchronized in your sleep at night and by sub-conscious prompting during the day with the help of your Guides and friends in Spirit. You may wake up with the idea that you should go to a certain place at a certain time. The person you are destined to meet may also have received similar cues and you meet, apparently by 'chance'. You may react with instant love or hate but it was not "at first sight". If you are not a spontaneous person or are overly cautious then synchronicity may be a problem for you. If this is the case then you may have dreams in which you are in the wrong place, too early or late or you miss the bus, plane or train connection. You can learn how to take advantage of upcoming opportunities for romance or business by understanding your dreams. For example, if you are destined to meet an important new business or romantic partner then that person may appear in your dreams – usually in the form of someone unknown to you. The dream may feature attempts to get to a meeting – e.g. attending a wedding or a business function. Usually, in such dreams you fail to get to the meeting – apparently through no fault of your own but this may, in fact indicate how your Shadow Self is limiting you. R-entering and changing such dreams can improve your work life or romance.

(C) THE CIRCUMSTANCES OF YOUR BIRTH

Your personality, health, happiness, wealth, 'luck', pattern of your relationships, success or failure in work or business are all determined by your reaction to your birth. On that day you decided what type of person you were and what kind of world you landed in. So, if e.g. your mother for very good reasons could not bond with you during the first 20 minutes of your life did you feel unloved or unwanted? If so, did you come to believe that you were a bad person if even your mother does not seem to want you? Do you, in present time suffer from depression as a result of that belief system? Did you blame yourself for the pain you put her through and if so, do you now suffer from guilt? Did you decide that the World was a cold, unwelcoming, dangerous place and what affect does that have on your present day stress level? Can you see how the circumstances of your birth influence your life? The only way a new born baby can get some idea what it looks is by interpreting the reactions of other people to it's arrival. If your parents did not seem to accept you to what extent did you accept your body? It should not be surprising that your dreams will have a lot to say about your first impressions of life on Day One. Incredible as it may seem practically every dream will relate to this first and most important event in your life.

How did you perceive the way your parents reacted to your arrival? Did you then and do you now still resent your parent's apparent disappointment at your gender? How does all this affect your everyday life, happiness and success? Can you connect your illness, your lack of success with work, the state or pattern of your personal relationships in present time with what happened at your birth? The answers to these questions can help you heal yourself and resolve your difficulties. Do you now transfer these feelings to other people in your life? You might, for example be punishing your husband for Dad's apparent disappointment at your gender. If Mum did not bond with you at birth it might explain why you have difficulty bonding in relationships and so on. Look out for dreams about your arrival (birth) at hotels e.g. in cold countries (your reception). Was the attitude of the female receptionist (dream language for Mum and the reception you received) chilly? Did the male hotel manager (Dad) turn his back on you or fail to lift your baggage (issues carried in from former lives)? What does all this tell you about how you felt then and how you feel now? Other dreams concerning your birth will have you crawling through narrow caves, getting out of elevators as the doors are closing around you or squeezing out of the narrow window of a house. Many dreams have you approaching a building (mothers body) entering, interacting with the people inside and then leaving.

Consider the following Dreams from two ladies:

"I was back in my parent's house. I was keeping a baby elephant as a pet in the box room. My mother did not know about it so I was desperately trying to keep it a secret. Inevitably, it grew too big for the room so I had to squeeze it down the stairs and out the back door. I was surprised to find that the back garden had changed. The grass and flowers were gone. I found myself in a cold, concrete back yard“.

Interpretation:

By re-entering this dream and having a conversation with the baby elephant the dreamer realized that her mother did not welcome the pregnancy, She herself was a sensitive and loving soul, but because of the birth she had become emotionally hardened (developed a tough skin like an elephant). This hardness buried the love (flowers in the garden) and turned her blood (the grass) cold. The cemented back yard like a wall indicates an emotional protective covering which can negatively affect her heart and circulatory system.

(2)

“I visited my mother. I had not seen her for a long time. When I arrived she was dead – lying on a cold, marble slab. My father blamed me for something. Mrs. Murphy, a neighbor put her arm around me and told me I look well”.

Interpretation:

In a similar fashion to (1) this dreamer hardened herself because her mother could not bond with her at birth and seemed to be dead (unresponsive). List "dead", "cold" "marble slab" "blame" under "I am" or "think I am." She also blames herself for the state of her mother. Solid things like the slab and the back garden in (1) refer to the dreamer's physical body in present time. Their descriptions in these dreams can indicate possible issues with the circulatory system.

(D) THE ROLES PEOPLE PLAY

As you can see from the two examples above the re-birthing dimension of dreams invariably indicates how the dreamers – in response to how they feel they were received into the World have assumed a false persona (Shadow Self), personality or role which they will act out throughout their lives even though it can create stress and predictable illness. There are a number of such roles. Some can produce cancer, others cardiac conditions, arthritis, and so on. In the above cases the thick skin, cold slab and cemented yard all suggest the role which we call 'The Aloof.' – a person cut off from emotions. I shall say more about how illness and issues can be healed or avoided by changing these personality types or roles. (See Chapters 18-20.)

(E) MALE AND FEMALE ASPECTS

The male hemisphere of the brain in both men and women helps us to be more managing, controlling, assertive, intellectual, decisive, courageous, etc. The female side encourages the caring, nurturing, accepting, forgiving, loving but also psychic, intuitive aspect of ourselves. These two aspects balance our energy to create good health and a well rounded personality. The Chinese call this the yin (female) and yang (male) side of our nature.

If you are too female you may over-react to trivial issues or events. If you are too male you may find yourself over-controlling or repressing your emotions. Both reactions can result in stress and illness. This duality extends to the endocrine system where there are male glands secreting male hormones and female glands secreting female hormones. The importance of getting the balance correct in relation to your gender is vital to your continued good health. Dreams can be very helpful here. This balancing and harmonizing can appear as people dancing in step, members of a band or orchestra playing in tune, etc. Generally, the male aspect is indicated by phallic symbols e.g. rods, poles, rifles, etc. while the female will appear as containers e.g. jugs, bath tubs, basins, etc. How the above symbols are described in the dream can indicate the state of these aspects of your functioning or how you feel about your masculinity or femininity.

The male aspect can also appear to the right hand side while the female is often indicated to the left e.g. roads to the right and left at a T-junction. The energy in the right side of the body is male, infusing and outward flowing while the energy in the left is female, magnetic and inward flowing. 'Hands –on" healers can feel this and use the left hand to draw out negative energy and then infuse positive energy in with the right. Read more about this in the e-book 'Healing with Dreams in the New Age' by George Rhatigan (Amazon Kindle)

The Chinese practice of Tai Chi involves movement to the left (yin), movements to the right (yang) and then bringing the hands together at the solar plexus (centering or balancing the energy).

(F) LIFE PURPOSE

Naturally, people tend to resist the negative descriptions of themselves they find in dreams but it is only by accepting who and what we are that we can move on to who and what we need to be. That is the purpose of every dream and every life.

The Native Americans have a saying; "In the beginning God breathed out and the souls of men were created. Then God breathed back in and these souls began their journey back to the Source". Each life is an opportunity to improve and perfect ourselves and in the process move closer to unification with the Creator. This in turn can help the planet return to its natural Garden of Eden state. As we work on ourselves we are also working on the planet.

The Real Self devises a plan designed to help us develop one or more positive qualities which was lacking in us over a number of former lives-such as acceptance, forgiveness, tolerance, patience, love, etc. This is done by choosing a parent or parents who are similarly deficient in these qualities. We copy the parent/parents, develop the same negative traits and the resultant difficulties and illnesses which ensue help us to learn how not to live our lives. Ask yourself this question; "What good qualities were most lacking in my mother and father?" These are what you need to develop in yourself. In a nutshell, by being more like God – loving, kind, and merciful, etc. we get closer to eventual reunification with the Creator.

You also agreed to develop and use the natural psychic and healing abilities of the soul to help others. You will meet old enemies and people you hurt or even killed in former lives. Sharing your spiritual gifts with them allows you to pay back the debt you owe. This can help them to forgive you. We agreed to this kind of arrangement in Spirit before we were born but many of us lose sight of it when we get too involved in our everyday activities. You may not want to develop and use your gifts. You may have misused these powers in former lives or were punished for applying them. Some of us were burned at the stake as witches for this reason. You might prefer some other way to pay your debt. Your dreams will be adamant that your specific gifts are your 'passport' to spiritual development. Denying them or trying to avoid their use can cause you mental conflict and real physical illness.

(G) KARMA AND DHARMA

We all committed atrocities in former incarnations and, as a result we can carry a sense of guilt which can cause us to attract suffering, illness, loss and 'bad luck' into our lives. This is called Karma – the harsh, 'male' application of Law of Attraction (Spiritual Law). This is not punishment but simply cause and effect. It can be exacerbated if we are too male and judgmental of ourselves and others. The 'female' or more merciful application of this Law is called Dharma. This involves paying our debts and improving ourselves with love, forgiveness and service to others by using our spiritual and other gifts and talents. Our dreams will remind us of this choice especially if we find ourselves at a 'Y' junction and a choice of paths – one stony, hard trail over a mountain (the hard way to learn and pay our debts) and another, perhaps more smooth way by the sea shore the (easier, female way). Other dreams might involve male and female police officers or male and female judges. They indicate the 'male and female' application of the Law. For example, a young lady who was studying law dreamt that she was in court and the female judge was talking about "community service" and mentioned a "statute book". The Spiritual Law of Attraction or Cause and Effect has these two aspects called Karma and Dharma. This applies to us all – whether we believe in it or not. If you hurt someone you will bring similar pain on yourself. This is called Karma. You will also owe a debt to that person and must meet him or her at some future time to repay what you owe and seek forgiveness. If you develop in yourself the ability to forgive and become less judgmental then you can also be kinder to yourself – in which case you can pay your debt by being of service to the injured party. In effect, it is a choice between suffering or service.

This is not unlike the way a criminal can pay his debt to society by going to jail or by community service. The purpose of all this is to qualify us for a better position or status in the Spirit World. As Jesus said; "In my Father's house there are many rooms" John 14.2. In other words there is a 'job' and a place for us in the next dimension which can be better than that which we left to be born into our present life. If you were satisfied with your living conditions 'up there' you would not have bothered to reincarnate into this life. If you totally ignore your Life Purpose you may still unconsciously make progress as you suffer the trials and travails of life. However, if you leave this life as you entered it then at the death of your physical body you will return to the same level of heaven you left. There is no fiery hell – just different level of heaven. Unfortunately, if your consciousness has lowered you may even go to less desirable conditions. Your dreams will keep you informed of your progress. Look out for dreams referring to "qualification, exams", or mention of "graduation". The subject matter of such dreams will, most likely be your Life Purpose and how well you are progressing.

When we die we are not judged or punished for the way we lived our lives. God does not give us free will and then punish us for making the wrong choices. That would not be free will. However, we are all subject to Spiritual Law and hurting others will bring consequences in this or future lives. We all have an in-built process by which we seem to punish ourselves with e.g. Illness, bad 'luck,' etc. Moreover, if we, for example, murder someone we are 'tied' to that person and are destined to meet again and again. The person we hurt can take revenge or forgive. We, on the other hand, have an opportunity to pay the debt by being of service. This continues until we forgive and' release' each other. When our Earthly life is over we simply gravitate to a level of existence appropriate to our consciousness. This is like water finding its own level on uneven ground. 'Like attracts like' by the Law of Attraction so we will find yourself living with souls on the same level of awareness as ourselves.

However, we will only achieve our new status if we

qualify by having completed our Life Purpose contract. The many dreams about failing to pass exams or interviews, qualifying or not at University, difficulty satisfying officials at customs or border posts that we are fit to move into another country or coming to doors or gates can represent the transition.

There are places and conditions on 'the other side' much better than those on Earth and other places and conditions much worse. These were not created by God to punish or reward us but are simply reflections or creations of the collective consciousness of the souls that gather there. Your heaven' or 'hell' will be a reflection of your consciousness which you developed over many incarnations. "The Kingdom of Heaven (or Hell) is within you". These 'hells' are not fiery places but rather cold, dark, ugly and on a lower level while 'heavens' tend to be warm, bright beautiful and on a higher level. Souls on the lower level cannot travel up to these heights because the brightness there would be painful to them but those who live there can choose to travel down to help those below. The good news is that you can work your way out of these negative places by trying to help others on your level or below it while you are 'up there' or by reincarnation to Earth, adhering to your assigned Life Purpose, and benefiting from the love and good example you receive from parents, family and friends. Some souls choose to learn and develop through suffering or illness. Cancer e.g. can teach you compassion for others. Blindness can 'open up' your psychic vision and so on. What makes this planet a great place in which to develop spiritually is that souls here are on these different levels of awareness. They can mix together and benefit from this. All this is designed to help you be a better soul leaving the planet than you were coming in and so qualify for a better place 'up there'. Essentially this means becoming more loving, compassionate, forgiving, etc. and using your spiritual gifts or powers to help others. Each life can take you a step closer to God. Your dreams will indicate what is required of you in this regard. The positive characters in the nightly drama- the Healing Agents, will have the good quality you need to develop and the authority figures – the Guides will demonstrate what spiritual gifts you need to share.

(H) THE NEW AGE CONSCIOUSNESS

Lately, many people find themselves dreaming about tsunamis sweeping across the country leveling all before them or “it’s the end of the World with tornadoes and earthquakes ravaging the land“. Usually, in such dreams the only way to survive is to get to higher ground. These dreams can refer to the Age of Aquarius which has recently begun. This is a cosmic event and its influence will last for approximately 2,000 years. This particular Age is bringing sweeping changes. Structures which we thought were secure such as banks, governments, currency, businesses, the church etc. are under great pressure especially where there is a lack of integrity. There is no place for the guilty to hide. This is making way for a New Order – a Golden Age of Love and Acceptance. The Earth is exuding a more positive vibration and energy. This is a time when people begin to take responsibility for themselves in terms of health, spirituality, government, etc. The New Age however is having a painful birth for many of us. Depression, suicide and dissatisfaction are widespread. The things and activities which used to give us pleasure no longer do so. Time is ’speeding up’ and events are happening more quickly. Chronic illness, even in young people which would normally take years to manifest now develops almost overnight. On a positive note, healing ourselves with natural means can also happen quickly and working with dreams allows us to receive the guidance to cope with these changes.

The difference between this Age and the one that has just ended is that this is the Age in which love and integrity are essential. In the previous Age -the Piscean we could live without these qualities in ourselves or others. We could tolerate coldness in our relationship with our parents and partners. Now we feel deprived if we are not loved. We formerly thought we were happy-or at least reasonably contented with our lot but now nothing seems to please us. This is not unlike a child happily walking along a street until he comes to a sweetshop and sees all the lovely sweets he cannot have. This is very noticeable in the dreams of young people. Many see suicide as a way out. This will solve nothing. Openness, honesty in relationships, developing and practicing acceptance and love can generate more positive energy and make us more compatible with the New Age energy. All this can help raise our consciousness – "getting to the higher ground to survive" as we sometimes see in dreams.

People in this New Age are also very intolerant of war; the abuse of the planet and what some people call "the forces of darkness". According to channeled information, there is a governing council or hierarchy of Spirit Guides who concern themselves with global issues. At the end of the Second World War they had great concern about the negative state of the collective consciousness of the people on Earth. There was a fear that a Third World War could bring about the end of the planet through nuclear destruction. This was predicted to happen about this time. 'Dark forces' were very much in power so it was decided to encourage many 'aware' or developed souls to reincarnate in order to create a 'Force of Light' to counteract this. These 'Light Workers, got into positions of power, became teachers or leaders, infiltrated every aspect of society and spread the philosophy of 'Love and Light (awareness)'. It is having the desired effect. People are beginning to change and express their anger at the abuse of power by governments. This began to be noticeable at the changing attitude of people to the Vietnam War. The process continues. All this prepares the way for the New Age. Agreeing to protect and preserve the planet can be another aspect of our Life Purpose.

(I) REINCARNATION

The purpose of reincarnation and working to

improve oneself is so that you can be free of the Earth and move on to better 'places' or dimensions. Many of your dreams will concern themselves with these former lives and their impact on your present incarnation. Expect to find dreams involving foreign countries, old buildings such as castles, churches, monasteries or people described as "very elderly "or "dressed in period costumes", etc. People are always surprised by this because reincarnation is not part of our culture in the West. Up to the 4th Century it was an accepted part of Christian belief but resurrection (the dead rising from the grave at the Day of Judgment), was a popular alternative doctrine. The fact that there was only one word in Aramaic, the language spoken by Jesus for both reincarnation and resurrection and the various references in the New Testament to being "born again" added to the confusion. When the Roman Empire embraced Christianity as a result of the emperor Constantine seeing a vision of a cross in the sky they decided to end the disagreement. A council of the Church was convened in 324 A D. The bishops were assembled and ordered to choose one or the other. They opted for resurrection. However, in this New Age more and more people are returning to the belief in reincarnation.

References in dreams to your former sojourns on Earth tend to fall into two categories:

(1)

Negative lives when (a) you suffered trauma in the past life causing you to experience consequences in present time such as drowning giving you a fear of water in this life, falling to your death resulting in a present day fear of heights, suffocation causing tightness in the chest area or breathing difficulties or (b) negative lives in which you exhibited habitual traits such as intolerance, impatience, fear, etc. Eliminating these can be a part of your Life Purpose contract.

(2)

Positive lives in which you had (a) the good qualities you need to develop in this life such as confidence, faith, courage, etc .or (b) you developed and used spiritual gifts such as telepathy, clairvoyance, etc. even if you misused such abilities.

Re-entering these dreams can help you eliminate fears, phobias, issues and negative traits. Listing under "I need" as you consider the positive former lives can also help you develop your good qualities and special abilities.

Sometimes your dreams will take you to the time you spent between Earth lives in the Halls of Learning in Spirit when you studied and prepared for your present life. Look for references to being" back in school "- usually at your present age or mention of a "book". This is the plot or purpose of your life story. Here is an extract from one of my own dreams: "I was in a book shop looking at a series of postcards depicting different countries. My attention was drawn to the last of these which was of a scene in Ireland. ". When I re-entered this dream I was informed that, as is common practice I 'signed up' for a series of lives designed to help me develop the positive qualities I lacked and to meet again the souls I hurt or wronged. Because I was a leader and ruler in some of these lives I owe a Karmic debt to quite a few people. – more than I could possible meet on a one-to-one basis. However, I can pay this by touching the lives of many using my abilities in writing, teaching and dream interpretation. If I get this right then this can be my last life (the last postcard). It is a choice between qualification or re-incarnation.

(J) YOUR SPIRITUAL GIFTS

Dreams, or to be more exact the God-aspect that sends them, attaches great importance to the development and use of spiritual and healing gifts. Jesus spent three years healing people and preaching his philosophy of love, forgiveness and spiritual service to others. He exhorted his followers to do the same. "I tell you most solemnly, whoever believes in me will perform the same works as I do myself, he will perform even greater works" John 14.12. St. Paul lists some of these including "prophesy, healing and the recognition of spirits". He also emphasized that these abilities are from God. 1. Cor. 12.12. We could also add telepathy, clairvoyance, clairaudience, clairsentience, counseling, healing people at a distance or by 'laying on of hands', channeling, dream interpretation, music, art, culture, inspired writing, etc.

But why are such gifts relevant to life in today's World?

Here are some good reasons:

(a) Using your gifts for the benefit of others can be an aspect of your Life Purpose contract and can enable the Law of Attraction to work in your favour as you follow the path of Dharma.

(b) You can bring people to an awareness of their spiritual potential.

(c) You can cure yourself and others of otherwise incurable ailments.

(d) Troubled discarnate spirits and negative energy can be 'moved on from people, buildings or land.

(e) Resisting using your gifts can cause you to suffer mental conflict, distortion of your energy and emotional or physical ailments.

You have a spirit/mind which can function outside the body. The latter is just like a heavy overcoat which you must wear for the duration of your life on planet Earth. As a spirit you were made in the likeness of God. This means that you – working with the God-aspect of your consciousness can have supernatural abilities such as healing or extra sensory perception. Allowing this aspect of you to express itself in these ways can give you a feeling of what might be called spiritual well-being or happiness. If you persist in believing that you are simply a body you will limit your potential.

Some of your gifts and powers will appear in your dreams as follows:

'HANDS-ON' OR ENERGY HEALING

Look for any mention of the sun or gold, horses, high-powered cars or motor cycles, hands, touching parts of the body and so on.

DISTANT OR ABSENT HEALING

Dreams of flying horses, overhead projectors, posters, etc.

CLAIRVOYANCE

The ability to "see" spirits, auras, the interior of the body, events taking place in the distance, past, or future. Look for mention of the moon, silver, television sets, number 6, etc. in dreams. Not developing or using this gift can impair your eyesight.

CLAIRAUDIENCE AND TELEPATHY

When you 'hear' on a psychic level. Look for radios, earrings, large ears, mobile phones, number 5, etc. Not developing or using this gift can result in tinnitus or deafness.

INTUITION AND CLAIRSENTIENCE

'Inner' knowledge without either 'seeing' or 'hearing'. Usually indicated by the number 7, cats etc.

CHANNELING, SPIRIT RESCUE, AUTOMATIC OR INSPIRED WRITING

These involve the ability to receive information, inspiration or healing from other dimensions and convey it to others on the Earth plane. These gifts or abilities can be indicated by:

(a) the number 2, dolphins and other mammals because they can function on two dimensions i.e. land and sea

(b) postal workers, post offices, delivering newspapers, magazines, actors, poets, singers, musical instruments especially pianos, media people because they carry, speak or express material written by others

(c) cylindrical objects, drinking glasses, pipes, tubing, etc because they are channels

(d) talking to 'dead' people, bridges, helping entities to 'move on' because channels can be of service to 'the dead', and so on. Automatic or inspired writing can appear as unusual or 'magic' pens. You may e.g. find yourself writing with a fountain pen (fountain of knowledge or wisdom) and so on.

INNATE WISDOM OR HIGHER KNOWLEDGE

Dreaming of universities, necklaces of pearls – (speaking with 'pearls of wisdom') books, libraries, etc.

Other gifts include; Prophesy, Counseling, Spiritual Leadership, etc.

The following dreams are examples of how people were motivated to use channeling as part of their Life Purpose contract:

The first dream is taken from the autobiography of Saint Patrick. As a boy in 5th. Century Wales he was kidnapped by pirates and sold as a slave in Ireland. He was guided by his dreams on how to escape. But, even years later his dreams would not allow him to forget his true spiritual mission. It is written in his own words:

'And there I saw in the night the vision of a man whose name was Victorious, coming from Ireland with countless letters and he gave me one of them and as I read the opening words of the letter which was the voice of the Irish I thought I heard their voice and thus did they cry out, as with one month;" We ask thee boy, come and walk among us once more" and I was quite broken in heart and could read no further, so I woke up'. It was then Patrick realized he had a specific mission and subsequently, as a bishop brought Christianity to Ireland.

A man had the following dream; 'I am in a post office in Soviet Russia. I notice a green cylindrical pillar box marked 'letters'. The Post Master hands me a parcel but I refuse to take it saying; "I have no I.D."

(3)

Irene, a lady in my dream group had the following dream; 'I was attending a course. The instructor asked me to play the piano. I was reluctant to try since I do not play any musical instrument. It was a very unusual piano in that in place of the usual holder for sheet music it had a screen. I sat down and began to play. As I did words came up on the screen. I then woke up.' That was the original dream. I asked her to re-enter and change it. In the new version she read the message which was:

'TO BE AWAKE'

TO BE AWAKE IS NO MISTAKE

NO NEED TO BE FRIGHTENED WHEN ONE IS ENLIGHTENED

SO JUST LET GO AND BE IN THE FLOW

NO NEED TO STRIVE TO BE FULLY ALIVE

CAN'T YOU TELL – ALL IS WELL.'

Basically, it is the same message in all three dreams even though they are separated by 1600 years. 'Accept and use your spiritual gift – in this case channeling', Victorious the letter carrier, the Post Master, the cylindrical pillar box, the piano all convey messages. Patrick and Irene both woke up to avoid the message. The man in dream 2 refused to accept the parcel (his gift). Soviet Russia indicates how he represses free speech. Irene, who never channeled before was delighted to receive a message in her re-entered dream. Dreams ask you to "wake up", be aware and accept your gifts. Understanding and repeatedly re-entering them can help you to achieve your full potential, in all areas of your life.

Your spiritual gifts, like everything else on the planet are male or female. When the energy or healing is outgoing from the body the gift is male as in 'hands-on' or absent healing. When the energy or information is incoming the gift is female as in intuition or channeling. Dreaming of a horse (male) and cart (female) can indicate the need to find the cause (female) before healing the effect (male).

(K) YOUR HEALTH, EMOTIONAL AND PHYSICAL

Your health, both emotional and physical can improve when you take advantage of what dreams have to say about present or possible future medical problems and how to avoid or heal them. As strange as it may seem, every night you get a 'medical scan ' and your 'dream drama' then features images of what is or what may in future time be going on inside your body. Doctors or nurses or other – Healing Agents appear and set about healing you in various and sometimes bizarre ways. These indications and warnings of possible illness appear in your dreams in ample time for you to avoid the problem. You will be advised on allergies, diet, lifestyle, exercise and genetic factors. However, the most emphasis will be on developing a more positive mental outlook. Dreams often indicate how painful memories from your birth, early childhood or former lives can leave you with negative beliefs about yourself, other people or the World. These belief systems create stress, negative energy and consequently physical illness. Look out for dreams which take you back to your childhood home especially if they feature damage or neglect to parts of cars, rooms of buildings, people or animals injured in certain places, etc.–indicating specific parts of the body requiring attention.

(L) THE STRESS FACTOR

Dreams have a lot to say about the effect of negative thinking and stress on the mind and body. Stress is perhaps the greatest cause of illness in the modern world but because it is invisible we can easily overlook it or deny its importance. Medical experts define it as the 'wear and tear on the body as a result of stressful events which could be physical, physiological, psychological or socio-cultural'.

Rats put under stress in electrified cages in laboratories created cancer in their bodies. Other rats in cages which had an 'off' button which they learned to use lived longer and healthier lives. Something similar happens to humans who are given to negative thinking. Believing that one is powerless or that life is not worth living can produce stress and retard the immune system. The result in the long term can be chronic illness.

Dreams can help you to identify when, where and by whom you are stressed on a daily basis. So, if you dream that a man is present when damage occurs to e.g. the washing machine then when Rule 2 (cause and effect) is applied you conclude that the stress of trying to please your father affects your stomach (the churning action of the washing machine). Other such dreams might include "twisted-up or knotted tights or stockings (stressful colon).

Stress is not about what you do but about how you feel about doing it. If you do it with confidence it should not stress you. How you related to your father can be the key factor. His job was to help you to accept yourself and to inspire confidence but if he was lacking in this respect you may have copied him. Did he undermine your self esteem by criticism or lack of praise? Keep in mind the following;

(1) Stress has little to do with what is happening in present time. It is simply the bad habit of worrying about what might happen in the future or reliving the past.

(2) It is rarely about real life and is, for the most part your imagination (Shadow Self) working against you.

(3) Most people do not know they are stressed.

(4) It is usually based on a sub-conscious belief system e.g. "I must prove to my Dad that I can work hard and achieve material success." "I am a bad person so I must suffer/do good works" and so on.

(5) Dreams indicate that judging or thinking badly about yourself can create stress, toxic energy in your body and eventually illness.

(6) One of the greatest stressors is mentally trying to change or control other people or getting upset when they 'behave badly' (in your opinion.)

(M) GENETIC ILLNESS CAN BE CURED

Dreams featuring trees, tree lines, clothes lines, markets selling farm produce, seeds, potted plants, etc. will usually be about genetic illness. Cells die and are routinely replaced with new ones.

Question: If this is true why does the body leave defective genes in the new cells it creates?

Answer: because it was not instructed or re-programmed to do otherwise.

You might think that there is nothing the ordinary person can do about genetics but the appearance of such symbols in your dream is an invitation to you to heal yourself genetically. You can do this by re-entering the dream and changing it. The simple technique of re-structuring the dream to include two trees in the back garden of the family home can be very effective. One tree can represent the father's family line and the other the mother's. A 'gardener' is called in to find and eliminate the defective cells. These might appear as rotten fruit or deformities in the branches or roots and so on. When they are taken out or otherwise dealt with a message is sent to the sub-conscious mind that you want genetic healing. This process and re-entering and changing dreams has to be continued for 3 months which is the length of time required for substantial cell replacement.

The healing group which I facilitate has had success in healing a genetic condition called haemochromotosis. This is an over-abundance of iron in the blood and results in painful joints. The sufferer must get regular blood transfusions. It is quite common in Ireland because of the Great Famine of 1845 in which one million people died of starvation. Some survived by eating nettles. Ancestral memories from such times of poverty and starvation can also result in depression and eyesight problems (sadness and unwillingness to look to the future), obesity (caused by a fear of starvation, 'poverty consciousness'(fear of spending money) and, as mentioned above haemochromotosis which is a genetic compensation for the loss of iron in the ancestor's diet.

(N) WELL-BEING OF YOUR CHILDREN

Being a parent – especially a mother can be very trying. In great pain you bring children into the World, lavish them with love, spend a fortune on their education, clothes and gifts and then suddenly at the age of 11 they decide that they hate you or they get into crime, anti-social behavior, develop a chronic illness or even go on to end it all by suicide or drug-related mishap. All this comes as a great surprise. "There was no warning!" you cry. There was, but you were not looking in the right place. If, however as a family you were in the habit of sharing dreams at the breakfast table, you would know your children on a deeper level. Dreams open the door to a person's secret worries and give you an opportunity to help and advise. Your children's dreams may reveal abuse, bullying, depression, feeling unloved or how they really feel about their parents. You may have known them in former lives – not all of which were positive. You might even have murdered one of them in a previous incarnation and this time around you are paying your debt and making amends by 'giving' him or her life. This can leave a child with mixed feelings about you – a love/ hate relationship. You may feel that you really understand and love your children but ask yourself how well your parents understood and loved you.

A teenager who was being pressurized by her mother to get better exam results had the following dream; "A nuclear bomb had gone off (her emotional response). I was in a railway station. A voice over the public address system announced that victims of the explosion should take the cattle train (her intestines – literally carrying meat and manure) to the North (need for calmness). My mother was there telling me to hurry. We got on the train but a short distance up the track (after a short time) the train was derailed." Six months after having the dream she was diagnosed with ulcerative colitis –a stress- related condition of the colon.

As with adults, an illness or the potential to create one will appear in children's dreams. Cancer cells e.g. are usually shown as negative life forms such as rats, sharks, foxes, especially if they eat or corrode the body or physical objects.etc. You can help your children by getting them to re-enter their dreams. Doing this can reveal the psychological cause of the illness and stimulate the immune system to bring about a cure. Children are particularly good with this. The rats, e.g. can be asked “”What are you”? (A) “We are a family of rats” “What do you do? (A) “We eat into the fabric of a building and spread disease.” What aspect of your life does this represent? (A) “My illness” “What are you doing to yourself or what is ‘eating’ you about the family?” The child may reveal that s/he is self harming as a punishment for causing pain or disappointment to the parents. S/ he may be creating illness to get attention or make a statement about perceived hurt or neglect. When the answer comes the re-entered dream can indicate how to deal with the rats. It will be necessary to forgive all the parties involved and especially the child must learn to accept the body and all aspects of it's functioning. This can ensure that the illness or potential illness is stopped.

Children can also develop confidence by facing up

to their fears in dreams which can appear as monsters. Naturally the child will run in the original dream. However, in the re-entered version if he is encouraged to stand, face, talk to or simply point his finger at the monster then his fears will dissolve or dissipate. If your child is acting out of character, depressed, bi-polar or given to outbursts of temper, self- harming or violent attacks on siblings or parents then he or she might be troubled by unwanted spirit attachments or entities. This condition will appear in dreams as negative groups e.g. vampires or zombies invading a building. Naturally, you should consult a doctor but there is a lot you can do to help. The child could be encouraged to repeatedly re-enter such dreams and evict the intruders or call the police and have them do it.

When a child is ill with a chronic illness such as cancer or a psychological ailment, the parent can feel helpless. As a former hypnotherapist, I can tell you that this form of therapy can be very effective in speeding up the self-healing process. Hypnosis, despite the myths and hype associated with its name is nothing more than an artificially induced dream. By calmly talking to the client, inducing a gradual state of relaxation and visualization of a relevant memory or dream the therapist can encourage confrontation, conversation and change. 'Stressors' i.e. stress – creating' people, situations and things in the client's life can be addressed and dealt with, The ailment can also be visualized (or given a shape and size) and treated with the natural, intuitive ingenuity of the person in the altered state or dream. The Americans have a saying;"If you can find it you can fix it". For example, the child (or anyone who chooses to do this) might describe the cancer as "a dark mass about the side of a tennis ball" and then go on to indicate ways to reduce it in size. Naturally, s/he should also agree to take a fresh look at the painful memories that contributed to its creation. If s/he cannot forgive the parties involved then at least s/he may be able to let go any desire to get even. Acceptance can be a stepping stone to forgiveness. Most likely, you have already put your child into this exact state by reading a bedtime story. Children, even teenagers respond well to this so why not consider using this technique to re-enter and change dreams or simply offer helpful suggestions. The child may not agree to co-operate with any of this but you are still not helpless in the matter. In Chapter (9) I describe how a doctor was able to cure an entire unit of psychiatric patients using 'distant healing'. I found that this technique can also be very effective for physical ailments. (See also Chapters, 5, 6, and 14 and the e-book)

Giving birth and rearing children can be a challenge especially if a young mother also wants to have a career. It is important for her not to repress feelings of anger or frustration at the limitation mothering can bring. Dreams indicate that this can increase the risk of breast cancer.

(O) DREAMING ABOUT CHILDREN

Children in dreams can represent aspects of ourselves which are in need of growth or development. Like everything else in a dream they can be listed under the following headings:

"I AM" (NEGATIVE)

Look for children negatively described or acting in a negative way. This may mean that you lack maturity with regard to the subject matter -for example if the dream is about relationships and the troubled child appears at the age of puberty, If you dream of a neglected child at any age use the 3 M's technique described in Chapter 22 and ask yourself what happened to you at this age which limits you in present time. Children and especially babies can represent your hopes for the future. A dead child can mean depression – loss of hope. Babies can indicate your Life Purpose – your greatest responsibility. Neglecting them by e.g. forgetting to feed them can suggest that you may be reneging on your obligations in this regard.

"I NEED" (POSITIVE)

Positive young males can mean new ideas in relation to the subject matter. A boy aged 1 can also indicate your need to develop your individuality (See chapter on numbers). Positively described young females can mean a positive new emotional response is needed. For example a blond little girl can indicate the need to appreciate your femininity (See chapter on colors).

"I CAN BE" (EMPOWERED)

Babies and young children wearing or carrying precious metals or gemstones can indicate what spiritual gifts you were born with. A baby speaking words of wisdom or displaying an extra sense like a 3rd. eye (Clairvoyance), an extra long nose, (Extra Sensory Perception) large beautiful ears or earrings, (Clairaudience) can mean that you were born with such spiritual gifts.

(O) PERSONAL RELATIONSHIPS

Personal relationships are often the subject of dreams. Usually they focus on what 'hang-ups' or habitual, negative emotional responses you tend to bring into partnerships. These, of course have been learned from your first 'love affair' which was with your father or mother. This set the standard or template for all future partnerships. If your parents had a difficult relationship you may have copied this. Look out for pairs in dreams. They often indicate the pattern of your relationships – e.g. a cat and dog, a pair of badly matched shoes, two armies or football teams fighting for supremacy, two "boring old-fashioned chairs", two angry bears and so on. The above pairings would indicate the negative pattern of your relationships. Many couples can react badly to each other because of hurt or injury they inflicted on each other in former incarnations. Consequently they end up in love/hate relationships. You can re-enter any dream – especially one involving two of anything to discover the circumstances under which you knew your partner in previous lives. Were you destined to meet in this lifetime and if so why? What unfinished business have you got together? How many lifetimes have you shared? What have you and your partner to learn from the arrangement? What affects (good and bad) are you having on each other, etc.? In this way you can understand, on a deeper level the nature of your partnerships. You can also learn about aspects of yourself that you need to look at. If such information were available on your actual computer you would not hesitate to access it- so why not use your 'dream machine' for the same purpose?

An aspect of relationship dreams that is often overlooked is the negative affect that long-term partners can have on each other. If one is overly-controlling then the 'top dog' can drain energy from the 'under dog'. This can negatively affect the health of the other. Women, especially who tend to talk a lot and expect their partners to listen to every word can damage the ears, mouth or brain of the partner. This can cause the latter to develop deafness, memory problems or tinnitus (buzzing, thumping or ringing sound in the ears) as he sub-consciously tries to 'blot out' the endless chatter. His mouth area may react if he cannot answer her back. (as we saw with Freud's dream). If he feels threatened he can build up a defensive 'wall' around the heart or a build-up of mucus in the chest or sinus area.

Partners can affect each other's heart. Consider the following dream from a lady in her 40's. "I was a house which was built in the open plan – no interior walls. In the bedroom there were two hearths with 'blazing fires '.Two openwindows looked onto a beautiful garden of flowers" The dream is trying to bring passion, (the fires) openness, transparency, (the open plan and open windows in the bedroom) and love (the flowers) into her relationships and sex life. The dream also indicates that her present relationship or lack of one is affecting her heart ('hearth' is a pun for heart).

Here's another lady's dream: 'My partner was none other than Hannibal Lector – the cannibal from the film 'Silence of the Lambs'. At one point when I looked down. I noticed, to my horror that he was eating my stomach' When dreams are depicting negativity involving a male you should ask yourself "What am I doing to myself because of him? "(The 'him' usually refers to Dad and the partner because we tend to transfer old feelings from the former to the latter.) This dreamer is in danger of developing cancer in her stomach because of what is 'eating her' (repressed anger from a negative memory perhaps of her birth or early childhood) initially about her father and triggered by the men in her life. Two rats in might such a relationship dream might carry a similar meaning.

The following is a dream from a man who was suffering memory loss; 'I was walking with my partner along a beach. We came across a strange habitation. It was an empty shell and I knew that we lived in it. 'The dreamer should ask himself; "What am I doing to myself because of her?" (The partner?) He would realize that she was draining his brain by over-controlling and making decisions for him. Why think or remember anything when someone else will do it for you? Eventually he may develop brain damage ("an empty shell").

Here's another man's dream: "I was walking in an open park with a woman. Everywhere there were statues". The dreamer is not emotionally 'open' or honest about how he feels. (The park tries to create 'openness') He is also like a statue – cold and unexpressive. This can lead to 'hardness' of the heart and issues with the circulatory system. 'Statue' is a pun for 'is that you?' In other words 'is this the Real You – the best you can do in a relationship?'

Most dreams which concern themselves with your personal life highlight the advantages of positive long-term, committed relationships. Dreams involving two swans – which commit themselves to lifelong relationships can indicate this need. Such partnerships can have a balancing affect on your brain and positive effects on your glandular, circulatory systems and balance of the male and female energy of the body. Women living alone can become mentally unbalanced while men in similar circumstances can suffer depression. Both men and women can develop heart conditions from a lack of emotional or physical sharing of themselves.

Dreams suggesting the benefits of a relationship often have you preparing or attending a wedding and the various problems you encounter e.g. the bride or groom fails to appear, the taxi is late, plane or rail connections are not made, etc. These obstacles seem to be out of your control but, when you apply Rules 3 and 4 you can see that they represent your Shadow Self (sub-conscious) objecting to such a commitment. This may be down to conditioning from your parents or negative memories of their relationship.

In dreams the person you are expected to marry will usually have the quality or qualities you need to develop. So, if you are to marry an older person then this would seem to indicate that you lack maturity and so on. Look out for male phallic symbols such as poles, sticks, rifles, etc. and female 'container' symbols like baths, buckets, jars, etc. Dreams involving such symbols mean you may need to develop the male or female aspect of yourself. If these symbols are coming together in the dream then you need the balancing effects of harmony between the two. Consider the following dream; 'I was going to the shop with my husband to buy a bucket (my female aspect) and mop (male aspect) to clean the floor (get a better understanding – floor = understanding) of the relationship). He suggested a different shop and we ended up not buying anything – (indecision thwarting the attempt at balancing her energy).

If your dreams indicate that you are attracting a negative type of partner, consider "Cosmically Ordering" a more desirable one by a) changing your dream to include such a person knocking on your door and/or, b) write out your "Order", comma, put it between the pages of this book, put it under your pillow, and literally "sleep on it". The universe and the Law of Attraction will do the rest.

(P) SEXUALITY

The word 'sexuality' can be taken to mean your mental/emotional reaction to sex. This varies greatly from person to person. Sex is pleasurable for most people. For some it is like an explosion of emotion while others are less moved. This is often because of the emotions and memories involved. Some are sexually indifferent or asexual. Some are addicted to it while others are actually repulsed. Some are heterosexual and others homosexual and so on. Sex should be a natural and joyous experience but for many people it can be a problem area – as can be seen from their dreams. This has to be the single most dreamed about subject. Such dreams indicate that our sub-conscious, deep seated beliefs about sex determine how we respond to the act. Dreams concerning your sexuality often take place in bedrooms and usually involve animals – representing your animal instincts. Expect to find e.g. dogs tied or on leashes, cats locked up in a' press 'or 'closet' (repressed or closeted sexual expression), nuns, priests or monks, (abstinence due to vows of celibacy taken in former lives), being frightened by snakes in the bed or chased (pun for 'chaste') by a bull (anxiety linked to sex) and so on.

Sigmund Freud introduced the notion of 'infantile sexuality' in a lecture to his fellow medical practitioners in the later 19th. Century. Before that time, it was generally believed that the youth only became aware of sexual arousal at puberty. Freud explained that a baby is acutely aware of these instinctive, sensual feelings from the earliest days. If the mother is comfortable with her sexuality then the child can more easily accept his or her sexual role or identity. A boy's first love affair is with his mother. How they inter-acted with each other in his earliest days determines the way he will respond to sex and personal relationships in his later life. Similarly, the girl's response to her father can set the pattern or template for her relationships. In other words, the child is expected to feel sexual about the appropriate parent. It follows that if he or she does not feel this way towards the parent at this time then there can be problems with sexual response in adult life.

These infantile feelings are not like adult sexuality but rather a sensuous, instinctive response. Bonding occurs on a sensual level and is essential to our survival. Studies have shown that babies and children need to be touched, held and interact with their parents at a physical level. Indeed, infants who do not receive this attention may die or develop serious illness in later life. These early sexual feelings go dormant at the age of 4 and will remain 'underground' until puberty. During that time the child may not be sexually aware. When the feelings re-emerge at age 11/12 years they can be in the aberrant form. Dreams indicate that Freud was correct about infantile sexuality. For example, if a male child does not feel sexual about his mother up to the age of 4 then he may become homosexual or asexual (sexually indifferent) in adult life especially if he had a recent life as a female. If Mum or Dad had issues is this area these can be passed on to the child. If parent and child knew each other under negative circumstances in a former life this can also affect the newcomer.

Similar confusion about sex can be expected if the child was sexually abused in the early years when his or her sexuality was formulated. Traumatic events especially up to the age of 7 can deeply affect the child. The age of a child appearing in one's dream can reflect such events and their affect in present time.

Another problem can arise if sexual intercourse occurred when the mother was pregnant and she was unwilling or distressed when this happened. The child in the womb can 'pick up' her feelings, associate anxiety with sex and as a result develop an unfavorable reaction to it in later life. Look out for dreams which involve "rifles being poked through the letter box, the ceiling of a room bouncing up and down, male burglars breaking into the house "and so on.

If a dream concerns itself with your sexuality (or any other issue you might have) it is not telling you that you have a problem in this area – it is trying to heal it. Yes, dreams will even try to improve your sex life. To benefit from the healing simply re-enter such dreams and co-operate with the healing. Consider these two dreams from a recently married man:

(1)"I was taking part in a classic (old-fashioned) football match (relationship) between Dublin and Kerry. Standing at the Dublin goal I kicked the ball directly into the Kerry goal mouth (no foreplay). Dublin won 1-0"

(2) "I was the best man at the wedding of two women. One wore a beautiful wedding dress".

A woman dreamt that she was in bed with her lover. He got up to go to the toilet and, as could only happen in a dream he removed his penis and left it on the bed. She took it up and started to eat it (The dreamer's sexuality or sexual appetite is too much influenced by her male aspect i.e. the sex drive itself and "detached" from emotion – as would be the case with the previous two men's dreams.. The female side of one's sexuality is more emotional and sensual. The toilet is helping her to eliminate some of her male response to sex.

Dreams indicate that, sexual problems can arise from unpleasant memories from birth, early childhood or former lives. This can lead to negative beliefs about sex or sub-conscious rejection of your gender. The final outcome can be physical problems with the reproductive system. This can be indicated in a dream by a bed or bedroom described as "dirty" ("sex is dirty"), blood-stained sheets (sexual guilt), bed infested with rats (danger of cancer of the reproductive system) and so on.

Sex is inclined to bind us to the planet so when we get old and lose interest in the subject we can also lose interest in life. This can weaken our immune system. We become ill and die. To counteract this we tend to get a resurgence of sexual dreams in later life to keep us interested in staying alive.

(Q) THE REPRODUCTIVE SYSTEM

The threat of cancer or other problems of the reproductive system is a very common theme in dreams. Such dreams indicate that deep-rooted, negative, sub-conscious memories and beliefs about sex, gender, femininity and motherhood in the female and guilt or issues with manliness in the male are the biggest contributors to illness in this area. Look out for male and female symbols described in a negative way. Everything in the dream is an aspect of the dreamer so when a female dreams about "scrambled eggs" (the ovaries), damage to container symbols such as "setting fire to straw in a barn" or "throwing acid onto the child carrier of a car" (the uterus) or crows burrowing into the chest area" she should take these as warning signals. Men should look out for damage to phallic symbols, spherical objects, wing mirrors of cars, etc. The main danger here is to the testicles or prostate gland.

Parents-to-be hoping for a boy, especially in rural areas and being disappointed when a girl arrives are the biggest contributors to the problem. I have found from taking people under hypnosis back to re-live their birth that a newly born child is acutely aware of who its parents are and how they feel about the new arrival. If they are disappointed, the child may feel that there is something wrong with femininity or masculinity in the case of a male child. This can eventually lead to cancer or other problems with the functioning of the reproductive system.

The good news is that dreams can be an early warning system which can help you prevent the illness from getting established. Many of the indications I have mentioned can appear long before the onset of the illness. However, it may not be clear how much time the dreamer has in order to heal and avoid the condition. Re-entering such dreams, understanding the cause of the problem or illness and changing the dreams around can help in this regard. If you have been diagnosed as having the illness then, in addition to following your doctor's advice consider repeatedly re-entering and changing such dreams. This should be done even if you have only one such dream to work on.

(R) WORK, CAREER AND MONEY

This might appear sexist but in my experience women's dreams are mainly about relationships while those of men are more often concerned with work or business issues. Women can feel at a disadvantage in the workplace because of their gender and the stress this can cause may have contributed to the increased rate of breast cancer. For me this was borne out in the many dreams from career women I have interpreted over the years. It also becomes clear from the dreams of those suffering from this condition that sub-conscious issues they have with their mothers and negative beliefs about mothering can cause toxic energy to accumulate in the breast area. There may have been too many children in the original family or the dreamer watched as her mother suffered trying to cope. The subject of mothering is like a 'sacred cow' and many females cannot express how they feel about it for fear of being thought a 'bad mother.' The breast symbolizes mothering and can become a conflict zone. This can retard the immune system in this area and as a result the body can create cancer here. I will say more about this in later chapters.

We would all like to know how to attract wealth and success. Dreams are pre-programmed to help you here but stress is always a factor. Remember, stress is less about what you do and more about how you feel about doing it. The effect of stress on how you do your work is a frequent theme in dreams. Work dreams often take place outdoors and usually in traffic. Another word for business is 'traffic 'e.g. "driving too fast" = driving yourself too hard "traffic jam ahead" = blockage to business in the near future, "new van"- esp. if young man is driving it = new business idea or venture, "a cat carefully treading its way across a busy street" = go carefully and intuitively through this business.

Work dreams come under the following headings:

WORK ETHIC

If you work too hard, not hard enough or are often out of work then your dreams will usually indicate that you may have copied your father's work ethic or belief system or are trying to get his approval. He may have believed that "money is only made by hard labor", "work is for slaves" or "I do not deserve money or success" and so on.

STRESS VS. CONFIDENCE

People can 'burn out' and become ill, not from hard work but from work related stress. Stress has little to do with present time and could be defined as nervous anxiety about what might happen in the future or sub-consciously re-living negative memories from the past. It is based on belief systems about ourselves, other people or the World. Examples; "I am not good enough for this work. Being female in the workplace puts me at a disadvantage", "The World is a dangerous place" and so on. Dreams try to heal this by getting you to adopt belief systems which infuse confidence. – "I am safe I accept myself and others exactly as we are", "I am good at what I do" "I choose to have success, money, recognition", and so on.

TIMING AND INTUITION

Napoleon Bonaparte used to say; "Don't give me a clever general or a brave general – give me a lucky one". Dreams indicate that we can create our own luck by making intuitive decisions and acting at the right time and place. Napoleon, himself won most of his battles by his wonderful sense of when and where to do the fighting. The same applies to business and finance. Recording and re-entering dreams can help you here. Look out for those dreams where you are often in the wrong place at the wrong time. Dreaming about an articulated commercial vehicle can help you to use the male aspect – drive, confidence, etc. (cab) and the female – intuition (drawn container) in your work.

ATTITUDE TO MONEY

Many of our money issues come from belief systems which we 'carried in' from former life experiences. Some of us – especially those interested in the spiritual/psychic scene have been monks or nuns in former lives – have taken vows of poverty, chastity and obedience. We may still, sub-consciously feel bound by these obligations. Others may have abused wealth or exploited workers and carry a sense of guilt about abundance. We might have lived in dire poverty and so now we don't know what to do with money. Naturally, when we 'meet ourselves' in dreams wearing the clothing or 'habits' of such people, especially in inappropriate places, we will know where our money issues come from.

5

When it comes to success and abundance, especially in work, career, or business, it is important to remember that money or a "wealth consciousness" attracts more of the same. This means, maintaining a state of consciousness that includes gratitude and a sense of prosperity, even when circumstances ,may indicate otherwise. Poverty or a "poor me" consciousness, is a constricting state of mind that focuses our energy away from a state of gratitude and in turn blocks prosperity and the Law of Attraction. Through focusing on and anticipating a lack of money or abundance, we only create more of the same. Consider changing your "luck" by Cosmic Ordering and changing your dreams of the night.

What does it mean when you dream about winning the lottery? Dream 'experts' will tell you that such dreams are wishful thinking. This is not so. Lottery dreams try to help you to achieve the abundance you are entitled tohave. The key question you should ask about all dreams is: "What is this dream trying to do for me?" Remember, dreams are pre-programmed to bring abundance. The only factor preventing this from happening is your critical judgment of yourself. Do you feel entitled to have wealth? Do you expect it to happen? The response of people in dreams to finding, being given or winning money can indicate how they attract or repel abundance in real life. A man dreamt that he, with a group of others were listening to the lotto numbers being read out over a public address system. As each number was called a great cheer went up from the crowd. Unfortunately, when the last number was called it was drowned out by the crowd cheering prematurely so he had to guess it. All the numbers turned out to be correct except the last one. A clergyman had better 'luck'. He wanted money for the church roof and the correct numbers were given to him in a dream.

The consciousness and energy of the planet is pre-programmed towards perfection, love and happiness. Look at the way a flower automatically strives to achieve its greatest blossoming – for no other reason but love. The World was meant to be an enjoyable place to live. The energy of the original Garden of Eden still exists here on Earth with its facility to grant your wishes – in the words of the poet:

'AND ALL THAT YOU ASK FOR AND ALL YOU DESIRE

MUST COME AT YOUR BIDDING AS FLAME OUT OF FIRE'

Tieme Ranapiri

Believe it or not, our sorry old planet is trying to return in that direction – esp. in this New Age consciousness. This can be expedited if enough people develop a peaceful state of acceptance and tolerance.

(S) THERE IS NO DEATH

If the death of your physical body is inevitable the process of passing begins. Some of your relatives or friends who have passed into Spirit before you gather at your bedside. Their job is to guide you through this process. During the initial phase of this a doorway or 'portal' opens into another dimension. You must go through this within 90 hours according to psychics– a little under 4 days in our time – at which time the 'window of opportunity' closes. We have free will throughout eternity and you can refuse to co-operate if you wish. This can leave you stuck between dimensions. Similarly, suicide, murder or accident can put you in this state.

Suicide solves nothing. If you are depressed you may contemplate taking your own life. If you think that this will end your troubles you are mistaken – it will not. Invariably, your dreams will indicate what you can expect to find on the other side. Even if you have no real intention of killing yourself, simply wishing to be dead can bring dreams of being in dark places and nightmares.

Usually, in such dreams you find yourself in a dark city (negative state of mind). You left your car or bicycle (death of the physical body) parked but now you cannot find it. It has been stolen or towed away by the authorities. You experience a great sense of panic and loss and try to find your way home (proper place in Spirit). You go through endless streets and no one seems to be able to help you. You usually wake up at this stage – relieved that it was only a dream.

(T) THE SPIRIT WORLD

Many people, for a variety of reasons can experience difficulty 'moving on' when their physical life is over – but they can be helped. I facilitate a group of people who choose to work at what we call "Spirit Rescue". We regularly visit cemeteries, scenes of accidents and even ancient battlefields. We meditate as in Chapter 6, and protect our auras by visualizing ourselves in a 'ball of golden light'. Next we mentally 'construct' a lighthouse to attract the attention of lost or confused spirits and then a portal in the form of a tunnel or ball of light leading to a staircase or escalator. We then call on these spirits to think of a loved one who 'passed over' before them and who is now willing to help them enter the portal and move on. Incredibly, we psychically become aware of acres of spirits 'sleeping' in the ground. Because of their religious conditioning they are apparently waiting for the 'Day of Judgment.' Some are 'held' on the Earth plane because of the grief of those they left behind or by their fear of Hell. Others are there because they firmly believe there is no afterlife. We encourage them all to enter the portal in their own time. To end the session, we usually count using a method of Kinesiology to establish the number of souls we attracted. (For more details, see Chapter 22 and the e-book.)

People who lose a loved one by e.g. suicide, drug abuse or misadventure naturally feel helpless. However, they are invariably given an opportunity to help the departed loved one in their dreams. Some years ago I was contacted by a young woman who was surprised to have had the same dream as her mother and on the same night. Her brother was a drug addict. She, with others in the family took on the responsibility of minding him in case he self harmed. However, on one occasion he was left alone in the house while she went out with a friend. When she returned he was gone. Some days later his dead body was found at the foot of a nearby cliff.

THE DREAM

She finds herself at the beach with a horse and cart. The sky is dark and gloomy (her state of her mind). She knows that her brother's body is in the sea which is turbulent (the dark troubled dimension in which he finds himself). She has the responsibility of recovering his body (Spirit Rescue). She tries to do so but her fear drives her back. She wakes up.

Her mother had an almost identical dream. The

horse represents 'male healing' i.e. encouraging and energizing. The cart is 'female healing' — the receptive, intuitive, ability. She needed both to help her brother. I put her back into the dream on a number of occasions. Each time, she found him and gave him counsel and encouragement to move on. Sometimes the dream changed and he was in a dark cave system. She learned how to re-enter and change her own dreams and three weeks later she phoned me to tell me that he had 'moved on.' I was able to confirm this with Kinesiology.

The dark places in which people who commit suicide can find themselves is not some kind of judgment from a Higher Power. It is simply the effect of moving from one dimension to another without going through the proper procedure, and in a negative frame of mind. I attended a Catholic school and we were taught that it is good to 'pray for the dead so that they may be released from their 'sins'. The concept of 'sin and punishment' does not exist in the Spirit dimensions. Instead of 'sin', read '*negative state of consciousness*' and for 'punishment' read '*the consequences of such negativity*', But the Church was correct in that when you pray for the 'dead' you surround them with light and it makes it easier other spirits to find and help them.

In ordinary circumstances dying is a very pleasant experience like going through a doorway and into another sphere of life. Doors are a frequent and important symbol in dreams. They can indicate the ending of one chapter in your life and the beginning of a new one. The final door can sometimes suggest the possible demise of your physical body. A friend of mine, a man in his late 60's who was in poor health and hugely overweight had the following dream.

THE DREAM

"I was in a large room and approaching a door which a decorator was painting white. I turned away from it and went through a different door where I found a new pair of trousers hanging up beside a fireplace. I needed such trousers as part of a suit I intended to wear at a graduation function".

MY INTERPRETATION

The dreamer's "Life Purpose" was to develop the male aspect (to wear the trousers). He needs this quality for whatever he is expected to do in the next dimension (his graduation). The fireplace is to give him the heart (pun on 'hearth') to continue with life. White is the colour of perfection and is often used in death dreams as in 'going to a large, white mansion', or 'snow in Antarctica' (the end of one's World), 'white doors,' etc. Look out also for references to 'going home', 'end of the road,' 'leaving the cinema before the end of the film' etc. Usually, in such dreams you are given the option of staying or going.

9

HOW CAN I REMEMBER MY DREAMS?

Fig.3: Techniques to remember your Dreams

(1) Place a notebook with a pen attached by a string on the bedside locker

(2) Put a glass of water on the locker

(3) Cup your hands around the glass without touching it and imagine that you are watching a light moving in a vertical circle going into the water through your hands. Follow the light without moving your head – eyes only.

(4) At the moment the light enters the water make the statement: “I will remember my dreams tonight.” or “I want a dream about my new job offer or relationship (or whatever)”. Repeat this three times. Then drink half the water. When you wake reach for the notebook and write key words taken from the dream. (Do not do what the poet Beaudelaire did. He was inclined to get inspiration from his dreams. In his haste to record this, he would write it on the nearest thing to hand – the bare back of his mistress. History does not tell us what he used for a pen. He may have been short of paper but he had the right idea!).

(5) At the breakfast table when you read back the key words, the entire dream can come back to you. This is based on the idea that water has the ability to retain and project a program. The programmed water you drink and that remaining in the glass can transmit instructions to your sub-conscious mind. A similar effect can be achieved by programming a clear quartz crystal in the same way and placing it on the bedside locker.

Another technique involves pressing the meridian point in the little hollow between the base of your nose and the upper lip and making the statement as above. The same effect can be achieved by lightly pressing two fingers from the same hand on the eyeballs of your closed eyes as you again make the statement.

DREAM JOURNAL

Keeping a record of your dreams and your interpretations of them can be of great benefit. This can be used to focus your unconscious mind on helping you achieve your goals in life. Do this by writing out what you choose to do, be or have in a given period of time and why. Your dreams will give you advice, help and guidance on these ambitions. What negative effect did and do your parents have on you? Did you copy the pattern of their relationships? Have you 'picked up' a family illness? Have you become a carbon copy of Dad and married one of Mum? Are you blaming your partner for what a parent did or failed to do? Find the answers in dreams, record them in your journal and devise a 'Road map to Change'.

10

THE POWER OF MANTRAS

When you program water as in the technique described in the previous chapter, you will notice that it has taken on a gelatinous consistency. It still tastes like water, but the effect on it of your words and the imagined light has changed its molecular structure. This is consistent with the work of the Japanese scientist Masaru Emoto. In his book 'The Hidden Messages in Water' he describes how, by writing words like "I love you" on a piece of paper and attaching them to a glass of water, the water crystals form into a beautiful 'snowflake' pattern while the words "I hate you" produces ugly distorted patterns when applied in the same manner. This is important because there can be great healing if you learn how to produce positive energy in troubled parts of the body. Dreams indicate how negative energy can make you physically ill. You can change that and heal your body, mind and emotions using a positive mantra such as "I love you and I love myself", "I forgive you and I forgive myself", " I release you and I release myself", "I thank you and I thank myself". Remember, if you think negatively about yourself or others for more than sixty seconds, you will activate the Law of Attraction and increase the flow of negative energy. Therefore, it is essential that you train yourself to notice when you are thinking in a negative way, and learn to immediately re-direct your energy towards healing with a positive mantra.

In his book 'Zero Limits', Joe Vitale tells the story of Dr. Hew Len Ph.D., who found himself in charge of a unit of thirty criminally insane patients at Hawaii State Hospital. The energy in the hospital was extremely negative and assaults on staff and inmates were a daily occurrence. His training in conventional psychiatry was of no use to him, and he had no idea how to help his patients. However, he was recommended to use the ancient Hawaiian method for achieving wealth, health, peace and happiness called Ho'oponopono. This is designed to transform the energy in a building or a person by repeating a positive mantra. He and his staff used the following mantra: "I love you. I'm sorry. Please forgive me. I thank you".

I LOVE YOU.

I'M SORRY.

PLEASE FORGIVE ME.

I THANK YOU

This had the effect of improving the morale, self-esteem and disposition of the inmates to such an extent that in three years, they were rehabilitated back into the community and the unit was closed. Dr. Len went on to work with thousands of people including groups at the United Nations, U.N.E.S.C.O. and Hawaiian State Teachers Association.

It is important to remember that Dr. Len cured these people without ever talking to them. Ho'oponopono (which in Hawaiian means to "make perfect") is based on the idea – as in dreams, that troubled people in your life represent troubled aspects of yourself. Len would simply read the file of each patient and, in meditation, identify a fault or weakness in himself that he shared with that person.

Then, by repeating the mantra he would cleanse his own energy and release the habitual, negative belief system or emotion responsible. So, in effect he cured others by (telepathic) example. We call this 'absent healing' and it is available to everyone.

If you have troubled children you will understand how difficult it can be to communicate with them. But, learning this technique, listening to their dreams and honestly looking at and dealing with what negative belief systems and hang-ups you unwittingly 'passed on' to them, you can heal them. Patience is required. Dr. Len may have had a 'captive audience' but it still took him three years.

He, being a psychiatrist, naturally confined his healing to psychiatric patients. Similar results can be achieved with chronic physical ailments. I have found this mantra to be very effective in healing people by changing the energy in their bodies, in their auras and the surrounding area. However, in meditation it was pointed out to me that, while this mantra can be very effective, it should be mentioned that it was designed for unrepentant criminals so the word "sorry" should be replaced with "happy" – since most of us are 'sorry' enough. So, my version is: "I love you. I'm happy. I thank you. I forgive and am forgiven." These words can cleanse your energy and bring in the power of love, happiness, gratitude and forgiveness.

Repeating this mantra as often as possible during the day can induce a state of peace and awareness. This gives off a positive vibration and can bring health, good fortune and abundance. When this vibration emanating from your aura matches the vibration of what you have asked or prayed for, you are more likely to get your wish.

"I LOVE YOU

I AM HAPPY

I THANK YOU

I FORGIVE AND AM FORGIVEN"

11

DIFFERENT KINDS OF DREAM

PSYCHIC, PROPHETIC, INSPIRATIONAL DREAMS, SPIRIT GUIDES & ENTITIES

There are three types of dreams; the symbolic, the psychic and a third which is a mixture of the two. The first, as I explained are healing and guidance in dramatic and symbolic form. The second are psychic experiences rather than dreams and include visions of events taking place in distant places or the future and/or conversation and inter-action with parents, partners, friends, relatives etc. both living and 'dead', Spirit Guides and lower-class spirits or entities. These dreams can be taken more literally rather than symbolically. The third type is a combination of psychic and symbolic. An example of the second category would be e.g. when you dream about a plane crash and then hear about it on the news. The questions you might ask are : (1) why was such information given to me if I can do nothing to change or prevent the predicted event and (2) how can I get more information or clarity so that I can understand the experience?

When we sleep we never lose consciousness. We go into various depths of altered awareness and continue to use our minds. In the shallow levels of sleep we dream for approximately 20 – 30 minutes and then drift into deeper levels. At this point we can mentally leave the body and function in what is called the 'spirit' double'. This is an exact replica of the physical body and we can use it now to' travel 'to other dimensions. Something similar happens when we die. We leave the heavy 'overcoat' we call our physical body and continue to exist in this lighter body in other levels, planes or dimensions of the Spirit World. While our physical bodies are still asleep we can go to what is called the Astral Plane. This is a dimension close to the Earth which acts as a 'half-way house' or meeting place between discarnate and incarnate spirits. We can heal and be healed, interact with relatives and friends both living and 'dead', use, develop and share our psychic abilities, give and receive information and so on. Sometimes we return to our physical bodies too quickly – hence the many dreams about flying, falling or waking up with a start.

After 90 minutes of this we come back for another 20-30 minutes of dreaming during which time images and snippets of information or inspiration from our Astral experience tend to be mixed into the fabric of our symbolic dreams. Recalling them gives us some indication of what we were doing 'up there' who we met, etc. To recover detail and get clarification of the visions we may need to re-enter the dream. Let me give an example of what I mean. During my days in the police force I had a good friend called Jim. He was well known and respected in Dublin as a tough but fair cop of the rank of sergeant. He became seriously ill and during this time I had the following dream: "I was sitting in a large auditorium consisting of rows of seats with an aisle separating two sections. I noticed Jim sitting several rows below me in the other section. He got up and walked into the aisle. I stood up and went down to meet him there. I noticed he was wearing the uniform of a superintendent. He explained

"They have promoted me now". That was the end of the dream. Four hours later I heard the news that Jim had died.

To make sense of the dream I re-entered it. Anyone can do this any time after having had it. Basically it involves putting yourself into a relaxed meditation using deep breathing or allowing someone else to put you into such a state. You can use the technique described in Chapter 5 for re-entering. The person facilitating you should have a list of questions you want answered. If you are doing it to yourself you will need to memorize such questions. When I went back into the dream Jim explained that he had died and had reached the new level of spiritual development he had aspired to in his Life Purpose (his promotion). The auditorium represents the Astral Plane and the rows of seats and levels in the building indicate the grades of spiritual awareness and development. The fact that Jim was on 'the other side' of the aisle alerted me to the fact that he had died.

Another friend of mine, a French lady living in Ireland had the following dream on the night of 12 November, 2015. "I saw men with bombs and guns creeping into a building and killingpeople. I knew I had to walk a path through the dead bodies". The next day she was horrified to learn of the mass killings in Paris by Islamic extremists. She asked me why she had this dream since she was powerless to notify authorities or prevent it. I explained that clairvoyance (The ability to psychically 'see' events happening at a distance) and prophesy (to see the future) are expressions of her soul and using them can be part of her spiritual contract or Life Purpose – ("Her path through the bodies" = her way to the souls of those who died.) The word 'psychic' comes from the Greek and literally means 'of the soul'. If she continues to resist this she can experience similar horrific dreams and mental conflict between her Real Self and the logical conscious mind. This can lead, in the long term to brain damage or eyesight problems. I also explained that she is not as helpless as she thinks. In the same way in which I was able to re-enter my dream and telepathically contact my friend Jim, she could communicate with any of the terrorists and try to deter him from his intended act. It may well have been that someone managed to do this because in fact one of the bombers changed his mind and abandoned his suicide vest. I also explained that she could contact one or more of the 'dead' people and help them to accept the situation and 'move on' to the Spirit

Plane. Dying in such traumatic circumstances or in the case of suicide can cause the spirit to be tied to the place. Such people can need our help.

When a friend, a relative or more usually a spouse dies the bereaved can often dream about that person. Usually the departed spirits look well, simply smile and say nothing. If they appear troubled it can mean that they need help. This is typical of psychic dreams. They appear to be pointless and contain no symbols or puns. This is because the initial contact was on the Astral Plane where communication is telepathic. The dream is simply a half-remembered snippet from that meeting. To recover the message it may be necessary to re-enter the dream. It's interesting to see how the images of such souls can change with the passage of time. If it was a long time since the death the apparitions will often look different than the way you remember them. If they were lame or disabled in life they may appear cured. If they were old when they died they may appear young in the dream. This is because if we die young we age in Spirit and if we die old we get younger. So, we all end up in our prime – apparently about 35 years old. When they smile or their illness or disability is gone it can mean that they are happy where they are and have resolved their issues. If they seem troubled or distressed then they may have left unfinished business and have not settled 'up there.'

A colleague of mind from my days in the police force had a dream about his father-in-law who had recently died and my friend was preparing to go to the funeral. The latter was a difficult, contrary old man who was cared for by his daughter. In the dream he was wearing a grey suit and simply said "Tell her I got the letter and it is O.K." When my friend arrived at the funeral home he was surprised to see that the dead man was laid out wearing the same grey suit he had on in the dream. He told his sister-in-law about the dream. She was shocked and tearfully related how she had come to the end of her tether with her tyrannical father. She lost her temper and they had a flaming row. That night he died. She was remorseful and wrote a letter of apology to him which she secretly placed in the inside pocket of his suit. She told nobody about this.

SPIRIT GUIDES

Practically all dreams contain authority figures such as kings, queens, princes, politicians, psychics, healers, drivers of taxis, buses, trains, waiters, librarians and so on. Indeed, anyone with a title or occupation or who speaks with authority can fit into this category. On one level they represent your soul (Real Self) but they can – at the same time symbolize your actual Spirit Guides. These are advanced souls whose job it is to facilitate you to carry out your Life Purpose agreement. They meet with you on the Astral Plane during your sleep and prompt you (telepathically 'plant' ideas in your head) during your waking hours. They are experts in their fields and will help you with the work you agreed to undertake. The occupation they appear to have in the dream or what they are doing can indicate your talents or abilities. So, e.g. if you dream about a writer or a poet then you may have this ability whether you know it or not.

Inventors, artists, writers and composers have been inspired by their Guides in dreams. Poets and musicians often refer to this spirit of their inspiration as the 'muse' – from which we get the word 'music. The musician Michael Jackson, in a legal action about a copyright issue gave evidence in court that he got all his music from his dreams. It was dictated to him and he simply wrote it all down when he woke up. In a similar fashion the sewing machine was invented by its creator dreaming about a phalanx of knights holding out their lances – the tops of which were perforated. This gave him the idea to put the hole in the pointed end of the needle rather than in the blunt end which had not worked for him.

Marion Herbert is a Dublin housewife, mother and grandmother but she is also an inspired artist and can psychically 'see' the face of a Spirit Guide transposed over the face of anyone who sits for her. She makes beautiful color portraits of these Guides but also of parents, ancestors and friends who have passed on to the spirit world. The features on the faces are detailed and life like and instantly recognizable. Marion needs only the name of the person on Earth who would like a portrait in order to find the link with their spirit friends, loved ones and Guides. People write to her from all over the world or contact her by phone. As always, these spirit friends have free will and it is they who decide who appears. When they do they can bring great love and consolation for people. (To view some of her portraits you can find Marion on Instagram : @Marion.Herbert.714)) She has had this ability since the age of four and at school she would paint religious icons to the delight of her teachers who deemed her to be a 'child prodigy'. She agreed to draw some of the various illustrations in this book.

Many people have a number of Spirit Guides – eight or nine is not unusual but you may attract more depending on what kind of work or service you do. Counselors or dream interpreters need a lot of Guides and spirit helpers who have expertise in many areas or aspects of life. Healers and therapists will attract Guides who were doctors or nurses in Earthly life and so on. One Guide called the Gatekeeper will usually stay with you for life or at least until you evolve to a higher level of awareness. The others come and go and share their talents with other people. One will be there for your protection (Guardian Angel), another financial advisor, another to inspire writing, music or artistic expression and so on. There will even be a Guide to help you find a parking spot. They will not tell you what to do since to do so could cause them to share your Karma or bad 'luck'. Nor would they help you to do anything that would hamper your spiritual development. Instead they give you options and show you the likely future outcome of such choices based on prevailing conditions in present time. Guides come in various levels of awareness so if you do not like or respect what they say you can ask for a second opinion or a better informed advisor. You may even find yourself talking to an apprentice Guide. We all have to learn our trade.

So, how can we make contact with these wonderful advisors? Initially, you may need a friend or therapist to guide you into a fairly deep state of meditation (as described in Capter5). It is important that both you and the facilitator are in a positive state of mind. To ensure that this is so repeat the mantra several times before you begin. In the relaxed, altered mental state you can re-enter a dream and allow yourself to experience 'hearing' without the use of your physical ears, 'seeing' without your eyes and so on. The facilitator should ask you to construct a 'Triangle or Pyramid of Light' with lines of light coming down from the sun, entering your body and connecting you to the other people both present and absent. This can ensure that communication and healing will come from a high source and there can be no draining of your own energy in the process. Repeat the mantra again and then the facilitator asks that a Spirit Guide who will know the answers to your questions comes down in the form of a "radiant human being". The facilitator will have prepared a list of questions which you will put to the Guide. Begin with; "What is your name? (Pause and accept the first name that 'pops' into your head.) What is your field of expertise? How can you help us? What can you tell (name) about the dream? What progress is s/he making with spiritual development? Can s/

he expect good news soon about relationships, business or work and so on.

THE ENTITIES

Lower class spirits or entities can cause panic or distress in your waking life and your dreams but, in fact most are harmless. Examples of this might be when your dream has you fighting off ninjas or non-human humanoids. They might be pressing their bodies very closely to yours temporarily immobilizing you as they make sexual overtures. This latter class of entity is called the 'incubus or succubus 'and their attacks have been reported for centuries. This experience usually occurs when you go asleep in a negative frame of mind. You can avoid this by repeatedly using the mantra during the day and especially before you go to bed.

People who suffer from entities usually have dreams about negative groups or a number of people in a negative setting -e.g. teenagers taking your car and driving it away, intruders occupying your house and eating your food, the Mafia, gangsters or extortionists especially if demanding money, vampires draining your blood, nits or parasites in your own or another person's hair, ugly or unwanted 'attachments' to a building, and so on. Sufferers can have low self esteem usually because of feeling unappreciated at birth or having experienced sexual abuse in early childhood. This lack of respect they have for their bodies makes it easier for the intruders to get established.

QUESTION:

How can you know that you are communicating with your Real Self, your Spirit Guide, a relative or friend in Spirit or an entity?

When you re-enter a dream, which is after all a message from your Real Self and (a) it is your intention to talk to this higher aspect of yourself and (b) you are in a good mental state (by repeating a mantra or prayer) then you are more likely to be successful. You may choose to contact a Spirit Guide or find yourself talking to a 'dead' relative, friend or spouse in a dream. Naturally, whatever information or guidance you receive should be carefully considered and evaluated before acting on it. An advanced soul or Spirit Guide will never tell you what to do about a life-changing decision. Entities, lost or confused souls, if they appear, can be in need of your help and guidance. Like children some can be mischievous. Listen to them, help or advise them if your wish and then command them to leave. They must obey and the act of removing them can be of benefit to you and them.

More information on this subject can be found in the e-book “Healing with Dreams In the New Age”.

12

EXAMPLES OF HEALING SUCCESS

Many years ago, as a result of a fall my ankle was badly broken. Arthritis set in and I was out of work for some time. When I examined my dreams I discovered that I carried a lot of resentment against my father because of his lack of support or interest in me or the problems of my childhood. I knew from my work with other sufferers of this condition that harboring such negativity over a period of time can change the chemical composition of the blood and produce crystalline carbon deposits which gather at the joints and create the illness. (These often appear as broken glass in dreams). I concluded that this and the fact that he also had arthritis contributed to my condition, I re-entered my dreams and in the virtual reality of this experience I confronted him about his 'neglect' – even though he was long since dead at this time. I 'listened' to his explanations. I also learned that although he was a good story-teller he was inclined to be shy about public speaking. I realized that I also copied him in this respect and I would need to develop the confidence to publicly promote my understanding of dreams. In the course of these 'dream encounters' I forgave him and we resolved our issues. My arthritis went and never returned and I became quite good at public speaking. I also found that the 'figure 8' device used by Phyllis Krystal in her book 'Cutting the Ties that Bind' was very helpful. With this, you stand in a circle made of blue light and visualize the parent standing in another such circle. Then you see a golden light inside the figure '8' moving clockwise around the parent and anti-clockwise around you. If practiced regularly, this can separate you psychologically from the negativity you copied from the parent. In a final ritual in meditation you visualize the negative bonds that tie you to the parent and cut them. In a similar fashion I also changed the pattern of my relationships with females by Cutting the Ties with my mother. Because I felt rejected or abandoned by her I expected to be treated in the same way by female partners so I tended to reject them first. When I realized what I was doing I changed this and as a result developed better relationships with women.

PROTECTION AGAINST NEGATIVE INFLUENCES

The figure '8' referred to above is an ancient symbol consisting of two 'magic' circles. This device can also be used for protection against negative entity influences and sends a message to your sub-conscious mind that you want your boundaries established and respected. This is a very powerful symbol and can even be used to remove curses as indicated by the following two cases.

(1)

The first involves an old friend of mine. He was very interested in Native American culture. He travelled to the U.S. and made friends with their tribal elders, shamans, medicine men and witch doctors". He had a dispute with one of these and on his return to Ireland became ill. He found that he could not swallow solid food and was living on pints of stout. When he came to see me he had lost 6 stone. I put him into the altered state and asked him to imagine standing in one circle of the figure '8'. I commanded whoever was sending him the curse to appear in the other. Contrary to our expectations it was not the 'witch doctor' we expected to see but one of his entourage. After two weeks of using the figure '8' he was able to eat and was soon returned to good health.

(2)

The second case involved a young man whose job took him to India. When he returned he suffered appalling 'bad luck' in that he lost his job, house and all his money. He came to our healing group saying that he believed he was cursed. I asked him for a dream and he related a recurring one in which he was "stalked by a black panther". I put him back into the dream and got him to confront the panther in the figure '8'. In 'conversation' with this creature which symbolized the curse or spell the full story came out. The man, although he had a wife in Ireland 'trifled' with the affections of a native girl. This was taken seriously by her parents who apparently put him under the curse. Once again, a few weeks of using the figure '8' brought him a complete change of fortune. Whether you consciously believe in curses or not – if your subconscious believes in them you can be vulnerable.

DREAM RE-ENTRY

A male member of our healing group uses dream re-entry to good effect. Recently, after having had surgery he contracted a 'super-bug' in his leg. I asked him if he had a dream and he told me the following; "I was looking at an elevator and it was swarming with bugs which were flying around and going in and out of the elevator doors". By repeating the mantra he put himself into the relaxed, meditative state and re-entered the dream. He immediately realized that this was the hospital elevator and that it was here he contracted the illness. I asked him how he should change the dream and he suggested calling the Fire Brigade. They came out and hosed the elevator with foam, taking care to kill every bug. Very shortly after this his illness went and never returned.

We found that the system described above of re-entering and changing dreams was very effective with cancer sufferers and recently we facilitated in the remission of cancer of the ovaries, cervix, breast and liver. I describe the process involved in doing this in greater detail in the e-book. It should be said that these people were also being treated with orthodox medicine except in the above mentioned case of liver cancer. The man who had this was written off by his doctors and was told that he had 12 months to live. He has since been given the "all clear".

DREAMS AND CANCER

Cancer should not be a 'sacred cow' that cannot be touched except by professionals. Cancer patients and their loved ones can feel helpless when this condition is diagnosed. Of course, they should take advice and treatment from the medical profession. But they should also do all that they can to facilitate the body of the patient to self-heal by reducing negativity in their lives. They can do this by helping the sufferer understand, re-enter and change dreams. In my experience, cancer, like all other chronic ailments is created by a pattern of negative thinking, beliefs and emotion. It follows therefore that reversing this pattern can bring positive effects. The least that it can do is to 'buy time' on the planet.

EXAMPLES

(1)

Barbara, a woman in the group asked us to send absent healing to her grand-niece aged 18 months who was diagnosed with a tumor on her foot. I put the same man who healed himself of the super-bug into the altered state and by using Barbara as a link he was able to telepathically connect with the little girl. We directed the collective healing energy of the group at the cancer, the process of which he described as like 'sand blasting it'. The next day the tumor was gone leaving only a 'wine mark' like a birth defect.

(2)

Andrea was another member of a healing group I facilitated. One day she rang me in a state of panic. She had discovered a lump on her breast. She told me that she had contacted the local hospital but would have to wait three weeks to see a specialist. She was very worried because her sister had two mastectomies (surgical removal of the breast) and a hysterectomy (removal of the uterus). She came to see me and I used the '3.M.s' technique (as described in Chapter 21) to take her back to re-live memories which would help her to understand why she had the problem. She came from a family where the female siblings were 'second class citizens'. This, issues with her father and how she felt about her femininity and mothering came up as possible contributory factors to her problem. She also recalled an encounter with a neighborhood "pervert" who had chased her as she walked home from work in the dark. She agreed to neutralize or heal these memories using the technique and to put the figure 8 around Dad and the neighbor in turn. She did this and the lump had disappeared by the time she got to see the specialist. The sub-conscious mind is like a machine. If it is programmed to separate a woman from her femininity and make her body more man-like it has the power to generate negative toxic energy in those parts associated with her femininity and create cancer there. Andrea's dreams were very helpful to me in monitoring her progress .Once again, the importance of accepting the bodyand all aspects of its functioning was brought home to me.

HEALING EYESIGHT

I often use regression to former lives in order to heal people of illness in present time. A nurse in her 30's who attended one of our workshops asked for healing for her eyesight. She was color-blind and had 75 % of normal vision. I put her into regression and asked her to go back to an incident from this or a previous life which would help her to understand why she had the problem. She described a war situation in a life in Greece in which she was struck by an arrow in the side of her head behind her eye. It took her two days to die. She was asked to describe the process of leaving her body at the moment of death. This was a pleasant sensation of floating up away from the land and from the outline she saw that it was Greece. She was then asked to release the 'energy' or 'thought form' of that memory from her spirit body. This was described as an arrow still stuck in her 'spirit' head. She removed it and when the session was over the color-blindness was gone and her sight was 100% normal.

This happened at a two-day, Saturday and Sunday workshop. She was healed on the Saturday and told the group that she was looking forward to telling her nursing friends about this at a social event that evening. However, when she met up with them they told her that such a cure was impossible. Consequently, when she returned to the workshop on Sunday the cure (remission) was gone and she was back to her color-blindness and limited vision. She refused to undergo the process again and we never heard from her since. Some people have a psychological need to suffer in specific ways. She may have been sub-consciously using her limited physical vision to learn to accept psychic vision i.e. clairvoyance.

RELATIONSHIP ISSUES

Stephen travelled sixty miles to see me on the recommendation of a therapist who lived in his area. He was a huge, 'Schwarzenegger' of a man with bulging muscles and a macho attitude. However, he was reluctant to tell me what he wanted. To 'break the ice' I asked him for a recent dream. He related snippets from recurring dreams about the Second World War including a mention of "two tanks". From this I gathered that he had a recent military life but the two tanks intrigued me. Pairs in a dream usually refer to personal relationships and tanks are phallic symbols. I asked him why his personal life was described as 'male and male' rather than 'male and female'. This question 'opened the door' and he told me his story.

He was homosexual and only 'turned on' by teenage boys. He was in the habit of traveling to Dublin and meeting male prostitutes in steam rooms. This lifestyle disgusted him and filled him with remorse. He was lonely for companionship and said that if he could not change his sexuality he would 'end it all'. Like many in this New Age he felt that he could not live without love.

I brought him back to a "life that would help him

understand why he had this problem". He went back to his last life. He was a ruthless, Nazi tank commander and totally immersed in the male-oriented, Hitler Youth philosophy of that war. I brought him to incidents from that life which would highlight his personality. He was completely without mercy and had to 'blot out' his female aspect of love and compassion to carry out his orders. He died as he would have liked in battle. I then asked him to come out of his body and "move up to a great light in the sky". I got him to merge with this light, be spiritually cleansed and allow it to enter into every muscle, bone nerve and cell of his body – removing all negativity like having a spiritual 'shower'. He was then told to meet a Spirit Guide in the form of a "radiant human being" who would help him to assess the life that has just ended and prepare him for the next one. The Guide appeared as female and asked to be called Athena.

This is a device I use to help people relive the time in Spirit between lives and to get to know their Life Purpose. Athena brought Stephen into a room and on a screen showed him images of his life as the German soldier. They discussed his shortcomings in that life and then I brought him forward in time to when he was getting ready to be born into his present life. In answer to my questions, Athena told him that he was expected to bring love back into his consciousness. To that end he chose parents who would cause him to be sexually and emotionally dissatisfied. This would make him seek answers to what life was all about. On the screen he saw his mother giving birth to him. She became ill for sometime after that and died. His father blamed him for this and sent him away to be reared by his uncle. Because he could not bond sexually or emotionally with his mother and was rejected by his father he became confused about his sexual identity.

I was guided by these revelations as to how to proceed with the therapy. In later sessions I regressed him back to relive his birth. This was upsetting for him but I changed the scenario by getting him to bond with an imaginary, "motherly" female who would do what his real mother failed to do at the actual birth. This is a common practice in re-birthing dreams and is called the Healing Agent. This and several regressions to positive heterosexual lives had the desired effect. Some time after our last session he rang me from the airport to say that he was completely "cured". He was no longer attracted to boys and was going on holidays – with a woman.

CLAUSTROPHOBIA

A businessman asked me for help with his claustrophobia. He could not travel by air as the confined space of the airplane caused him to panic. If he went to a football match or the cinema he had to sit at the back and leave before the other people. I asked him for a dream and he related the following; "I found myself driving a horse and cart into a cave. As I was going in there were a large number of men running out. I soon discovered why. The ceiling of the cave was falling in. I woke up in a state of terror ". I put him back into the dream and he gave me further details. The cave was a 19th. Century coal mine and the cart was for taking coal out. He told me that this was a recurring dream but it always ended at this point. Now he realized that he died in this cave-in but because of his great fear he 'came out of his body' at the last moment. As a result his passing did not bring closure. He was re-living this death every day of his present life. His dreams could not heal him because he ended them too quickly. I regressed him back to that life and I allowed him to re-enact the moment of his passing. As he moved up away from the land I asked him to give the fear a shape and size and release it from his spirit body. This, he said looked like coal in his spirit body. I asked him to see this coming out of his body and falling back to Earth. To further help him I got him to practice putting an "image from that life" into the second circle of the figure '8'. It was easier for him to see this as a train track with a little train engine pulling empty carriages clock-wise around the mine entrance and anti-clockwise around him. He dumped more 'coal' onto these carriages. After two weeks of this, he was cured of his claustrophobia.

Regression, as above can be used in re-entered dreams as can progression which can be used to create positive future scenarios such as, passing the driving test, job interviews, special sporting events, etc. This works because the sub-conscious mind does not know the difference between past present and future. As you saw from the claustrophobia case, this part of the mind thought that what happened in the past was happening now. So if you enact a positive future event in great detail then it can think that it has already happened. So, it is more likely to allow the event to happen as you imagine it. We prefer to use it for visualizing healing having taken place and we have had great success with this.

DEAFNESS

A man attending our dream group who was

completely deaf in one ear related the following dream; "I was sitting in my living room when the door opened and two beautiful women came in. They made some remark about my ears – which I could not fully hear. I joked that their own ears left a lot to be desired because theirs were huge and like satellite dishes. They then reconnected my television set which was not plugged in and left." The television in his dream meant that he was clairvoyant but it being unplugged indicated that he was sub-consciously trying not to hear messages from Spirit (Real Self). Using regression and dream re-entry we learned that when he was young he could see and hear spirits but his mother would chastise him for this. We advised him to re-enter and change the dream by plugging in the television and 'listening' to it, practice putting his mother in the figure '8' and visualize himself fully healed. He did this and soon his hearing was cured Once again the importance of fully accepting one's self is an essential factor in healing.

SPINAL PROBLEMS

We have been very successful in helping people with spinal problems. Deep seated memories of Dad's apparent lack of emotional support can 'live' in the spinal area and cause illness there because the sufferer can believe that he or she is not emotionally or physically supported. We have found that re-entering such dreams, engaging in a 'dialogue' with the parent or person involved and putting the figure '8' around him or her can work wonders. Martin, a man in his 40' who was accident prone and suffered from chronic back pain is a typical example. He had a dream in which he was on a staircase with his sister. The handrail was weak and broke off causing her to fall to the ground and injure her back. Stairs or ladders represent the spinal column and when he re-entered the dream he realized that lack of support from Dad in his childhood had caused an imbalance of energy in the male (right side of his body) and female (left side – as indicated by his sister) causing a misalignment of the skeletal structure. He confronted his father in the re-entered dream and asked him why he had been so unsupportive. I used the same device that was so successful with Stephen which I call the Lighthouse (See Chapter 21 or the e-book) and allowed him to 'see' painful memories of this on a television screen and in the ensuing dialogue they forgave each other. Using the figure '8' he separated himself from the negative effect of these memories and his back and balance problems were resolved.

13

WHAT HAPPENS WHEN YOU SLEEP?

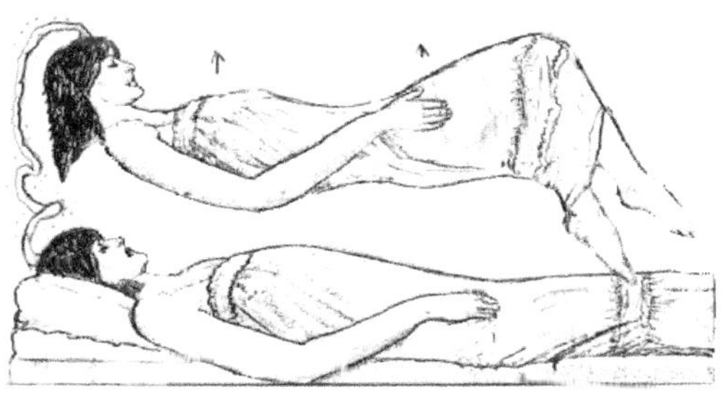

Fig. 4: Astral Travel during Sleep

The average person will sleep for 25 years and experience 300,000 dreams during their lifetime. We spend two hours dreaming every night but by morning most of us cannot recall what happened in our dream world. Those who do often attach little importance to it. But nature would not have devised such an expenditure of time without good reason. Sleep and dreams are important and without them our mental and physical health can deteriorate.

The routine and order by which we sleep and dream can be very interesting. Scientists, working in sleep laboratories have discovered that our eight hours of sleep is divided into four two hour sleep cycles. Initially, when we doze off we enter a shallow level of sleep. This lasts for approx. 30 minutes. This is when we dream. The energy in our brain seems to shift from the logical, 'male' hemisphere to the imaginative 'female' side. As a result, when we enter the fantastic world of dreams we do not find it ridiculous to communicate and interact with animals, angels or even inanimate objects. Our muscles are also locked. Nothing moves except our eyes which make little darting movements behind the lids. This is called 'R.E.M'. (Rapid Eye Movement) sleep. The temporary paralysis of the limbs is, apparently to prevent us from physically acting out the dream and perhaps injuring whoever might be sharing the bed with us. Some people who wake prematurely can be upset if the paralysis remains for a short time – especially if they had been dreaming of being chased and running with "heavy legs".

We then drift into deep sleep during which we can once again move our arms and legs and toss and turn in the bed. This will last for approx. ninety minutes marking the end of the 1st sleep cycle. We were not unconscious for the half-hour of dreaming and neither will we be "out of it" for the deep sleep period. The mind is forever active and it would get bored if it were locked up for eight hours of sleep. In a similar fashion to what happens when we die our consciousness in the shape of the spirit body simply leaves the physical body and travels at will throughout the Universe. This is called Astral Travel and psychics who practice it consciously can 'see' an umbilical-like silver cord connecting the physical body to the spirit body. This can be stretched to infinity but it breaks at death. We can interact with other spirits – both living and "dead" to give and receive healing, guidance, encouragement and support from Spirit Guides and friends we left behind when we came into this physical reality. In case we become too involved in these activities we are called back when the time is up for another period of dreaming. This recall can sometimes cause us a little shock and we wake up to the sound of a bell or our name being called. Sometimes, we are startled to awake with the sensation of falling from a height or flying thus ending our 'flight' from one dimension to another. Our activities in these other dimensions and memories of inter-action with our teachers, Guides, friends and other souls can feature in our next half-hour of dreams.

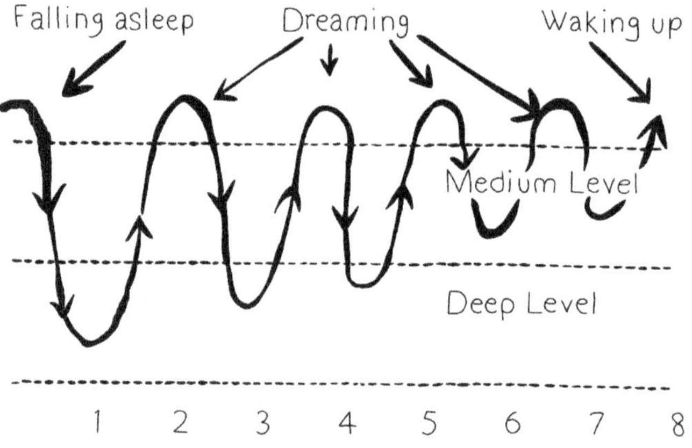

Fig. 5: Your eight hours of sleep:

four two-hour sleep cycles.

14

TRINITY OF THE MIND

To understand dreams and unlock the latent power of the mind it is necessary to know something about our mental machinery. The mind/spirit is non-physical. It existed before we were born and will continue to exist after death. Its physical counterpart is the brain which is divided into two hemispheres. The left side of the brain which is associated with the conscious mind is male, active and controls the right side of the body. The right side of the brain is the area of sub-conscious activity. It is female, passive and controls the left side of the body. In addition there is the wise and spiritual super-conscious (Real Self) which seems to exist outside the body but is telepathically connected to it. So, as you see, the mind is a trinity consisting of conscious, sub-conscious and super-conscious. These parts tend to act independently of and sometimes in conflict with each other. To achieve, good health and effectiveness requires harmony of all three parts of the mind.

THE CONSCIOUS MIND

This is the critical, rational, everyday waking consciousness. Its principal function is to interpret our experiences and make decisions. It has four qualities; imagination, intellect, memory and will. For example, if you were asked to go on a picnic you would (a) remember the last such occasion and recall whether it was pleasant or not, (b) imagine yourself on the picnic by scanning the future, (c) activate your free will whether to go or not usually by using (d) your intellect. This part of the mind is managing and controlling and puts up a defensive guard around the sub-conscious.

THE SUB-CONSCIOUS MIND

This is your own built-in super-computer which has overall control of the emotions, instincts, psychic ability and physical functioning of the body. This includes the automatic beating of the heart, the breathing, secretion of the glands, destruction and creation of body cells, immune system, self-healing of broken limbs and wounds, and much more. It carries the memory, as if on video film of all our experiences in all our lives in this and other planes of existence. This information can be brought to conscious awareness when access is gained to its long-term memory banks by relaxing the conscious mind with hypnosis or meditation. The sub-conscious has memory and imagination but little in the way of intellect or will. It is like a two-year old child in charge of a computer. It prefers communication in its own language – symbols, telepathy, emotion, visualization. Like a machine, it will act and react in pre-set ways according to the way it is programmed.

Some of this programming can be negative and counter-productive. Much of this was done by us in early childhood when we installed negative belief systems about ourselves, other people and the World. More came from parents, family, teachers in the process of which we created our personality – the dark, limiting side of which we call the Shadow Self. This acts like an over-protective nanny and can stop us from taking chances, commitment, – even falling in love. We need to update and re-train our sub-conscious from time to time. This can be done when the critical conscious mind is relaxed and access is gained to the "computer".

THE SUPER-CONSCIOUS

This is also known as the Higher Mind, the conscience, the God-aspect, the Real Self– or that aspect of us that is God. As I mentioned earlier, this soul aspect constantly motivates us back to the Source from which we came through spirituality, good works, art, religion, music, etc. It devised our mission or Life Purpose and sent us into the Earth to implement it. It does not, however abandon us here without aid or guidance. To help us on our way it sends us dreams to motivate us to be better souls and in the process come closer to God. Access to this higher part of our consciousness can be gained in the same way as to the sub-conscious mind.

A dream is a coded message sent in theatrical fashion by the Super-conscious to the sub-conscious. It was never intended for the rational conscious mind which can make no sense of it until the code of symbols is understood. The message is designed to subtly motivate the dreamer in a similar fashion to the way a melodramatic play or movie would act on our emotions. We wake up from the dream like members of the audience leaving a theatre- moved and motivated to change our lives for the better.

All three aspects of the mind can appear as actors in the drama but the sub-conscious has the power to instantly change the nature and appearance of the players or props. The Super-conscious, in addition to being the author appears as the authority figure (e.g. police officer, bus-driver, politician, etc). The sub-conscious, Shadow Self can play a negative role and demonstrate its objection to the process. The role of the bewildered conscious mind is played by the dreamer.

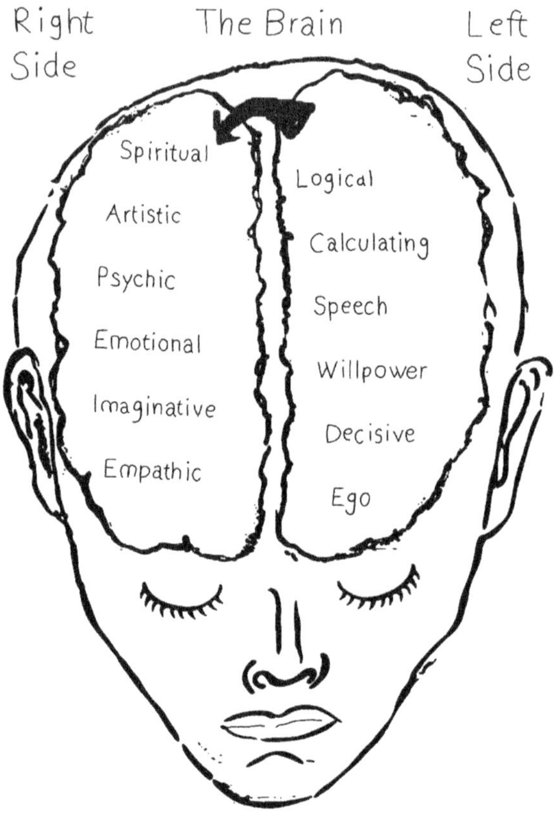

Fig. 6: Energy movement as we sleep.

15

HYPNOSIS, MEDITATION AND DREAMS

Hypnosis and meditation are nothing more than artificially induced dreams. All three are the same altered state of awareness differing only in the means by which they are achieved, the use to which they are put and the depth and apparent reality of the imagined experience. All three, even if the trance is not deep or realistic can be used as a form of therapy and healing as in hypnotherapy, healing meditation and dream re-entry. The hypnotherapist, in a soothing, calming voice gets the client to breathe deeply, imagine and feel his body gradually relaxing until he achieves a relaxed, dozy state that is half-way between full wakefulness and natural sleep.

(You can learn to do this yourself.) This is the same level of sleep in which we dream. The therapist then creates an imagined scenario which seems very realistic to the client. He is then asked to interact with heights, spiders or enclosed spaces (if these are his problem) and confront his fears about them. If he does this repeatedly, he can be healed – in exactly the same way that healing can be achieved through re-entered dreams. With hypnotherapy or dream re-entry, the client can be trained to stop running away or otherwise spoil the healing effort.

Hypnotherapy, like many modern therapies such as re-birthing, regression to early childhood and former lives, colour therapy, psychodrama, Gestalt etc., is based on dreams. Meditation is the same mental state, but is usually used for a spiritual purpose such as communicating with the Real Self or Spirit Guides, developing clairvoyance or the activation and use of other psychic or healing powers. The dream/meditation/hypnotic state is very useful because, by relaxing the limiting effect of the critical, rational, conscious mind and the over-protective sub-conscious you can expand the potential of your mind and body. Anything seems possible in these states. You can use your healing and psychic abilities, discover latent talents and powers, see and experience images from past, present and future, communicate with departed friends, relatives, get advice from your Spirit Guides and most importantly, connect with the wisdom and understanding of the God-aspect, or Real Self. If you practice these powers often in the altered mental state, you can find it easier to use them in waking life. If you lack confidence or love you can experience these qualities in a re-entered dream, meditation or hypnotic state. This can make it easier for you to develop them in everyday life.

As a therapist, I used hypnosis to answer life's eternal questions; "Why am I ill? Why do I have problems with relationships? Why am I unable to achieve my full potential? Why was I born?". These questions are answered with wisdom far beyond one's reach in everyday waking consciousness. By using hypnotic regression, I have brought many people back in time to relive the circumstances of their birth and the descriptions of the experience were remarkably similar. Most told of the pain of birth, the coldness and glaring bright lights of the delivery room and various other difficulties. Many recounted tragic stories of mother's failure to bond in a loving and accepting way with this new arrival. I learned how this initial rejection can color a child's image of itself and lead to serious problems in later life.

The usual scenario was a feeling of being unwanted and unloved because there were already too many in the family or, most commonly because a girl arrived when a boy would have been preferred. In the latter case, such a female child can quickly develop a negative view of her femininity which often leads to adult difficulties in relationships as well as gynecological problems. In the case of twins one may be hurriedly put aside while the birth of the other is attended to. This can leave the first born disconnected and emotionally feeling out on a limb. Unfortunately, these feelings can remain for the rest of the child's life. Problems can also be caused by the father displaying a state of nervous inability to cope with his new responsibility. The child, sensing this insecurity can develop a similar state within itself.

Some people bitterly described how, on that first day of their lives, their father attended to mother before looking at them. This, to an ultra-sensitive newborn, can be taken as rejection. The infant has a limited ability to rationalize and these early experiences of insecurity and rejection can form part of its image of itself. Our personality is formed by our interpretation of events on Day One.

DREAMS AND BIRTH

My initial reaction to all of this was one of skepticism. I could not believe that a new-born infant is so aware and sensitive. This is where dreams entered the equation because those same people who were reliving, under hypnosis, the circumstances of their birth, were also relating their dreams to me. Their dreams confirmed their accounts under hypnosis. I discovered that practically every dream reflects the impressions formed at birth.

Dreams constantly take us back to symbolically re-enact this important event. Dreamer's accounts of crawling through caves, tunnels, narrow gaps, hanging out of ropes, being lifted by the legs and subjected to critical examination by parental-type figures, were remarkably consistent with the accounts under hypnosis of what happened at birth. The dreams related experiences at birth, in the womb, and in Spirit prior to coming into the fetus and were consistent with their memories under hypnotic regression.

Dreamers tell of the study and preparation each one of us makes in the Spirit dimension in what they call the "Halls of Learning" before we enter the fetus. We are asked to accept a Life Purpose or vocation. We learn how this Life Purpose relates to unfinished business in former incarnations in the Earth. This aspect of dreams and hypnosis intrigued me but did not, as yet explain how quite ordinary people with moderate intelligence could gain access to great depths of wisdom while in the hypnotic/meditative/dream state – an understanding and awareness which years of conventional psychotherapy could not reveal.

I was later to learn that this wisdom comes from the God-aspect or Real Self which inspires dreams. I was convinced that dreams confirmed not only that accounts of past-lives described under hypnosis were true but also had a relevance to the way the individual lives in present time. For example, a sufferer of claustrophobia may have been suffocated or died in the cave-in of a mine in a previous life. At the end of each account of a former life the subject usually described floating up out of the body, towards a great Light, at the moment of death. Once in the Light the subject meets his or her Spirit Guide/guardian angel who with great wisdom and gentleness helps the person who is now in his or her spirit body evaluate the life that had just ended and to come to terms with its passing. But, what can we learn from this?

I learned that the mind/spirit can exist and function outside the body – even in a baby whose brain, scientists tell us, is like watery jelly.

I learned how important it is for the mother to bond with her baby in the first 20 minutes. If the child is taken away from her for medical or other reasons she should telepathically bond with it.

I learned that people can be healed from a distance and much, much, more.

Dreams constantly remind us of our Life Purpose and how patterns of negative emotions like greed, intolerance and hatred caused us to commit atrocities in former lives. We are shown what the future outcome can be in this life if we continue with this negativity. We are asked to look at "the big picture" – where we came from, where we are and where we are going.

16

LOCATIONS AND OTHER SYMBOLS

The following is a ‘rough, approximate’ guide to the more common dream locations which usually indicate the probable subject matter of the dream.

AIRPORT – departure.

NEW PROJECT, arrival – Birth.

ARENA, War, Scene of conflict – At war with yourself.

ART GALLERY – Ideals.

BACK GARDEN – The past, colon, elimination.

BANK – Energy, sharing, the heart.

BEDROOM – Sex, reproductive system, rest, meditation, astral travel.

BATHROOM – Puritanical attitude, need to cleanse the blood, action of liver and kidneys – especially if there is trouble with bath, sink etc.

BOUTIQUE or CARPARK- A choice of roles or attitudes.

BUILDING OR HOUSE – your body or that of mother at your birth.

BRIDGE – Ability or need to unite male and female aspect, ability to harmonize others. Channeling information or healing from the Spirit Plane. – helping lost or confused souls.

CEMETERY – Despair or change.

CHURCH – Spirituality, idealism, philosophy of life.

COLD COUNTRY – Emotional coldness, cold reception at birth.

CORRIDOR or LANDING – Transition, lack of commitment.

COURTROOM – Judging yourself.

DENTIST – Healing of your aggression or bite, animal instincts

DINING ROOM – Communication, inter-action and / or its effect on digestion.

DOWNSTAIRS – Physical, emotional.

DRIVING or MOVING UPWARDS – Rising towards ideals, activating the mental / spiritual aspects, raising your consciousness.

DRIVING with a family member – carrying the influence of the family.

CROSSROADS – Trouble and / or suffering.

GOING TOO FAST (especially uphill) – Stress –driving yourself too hard.

FARM, COUNTRYSIDE, ZOO –Basic, animal instincts, sexual, emotional aspects.

FLYING – Telepathically leaving your body, traveling to and from the Astral plane, rationalizing a problem from a more objective viewpoint or needing to ground yourself.

FLYING DOWN/ LANDING – Rebirthing or practical application of an idea.

FOOTBALL OR TENNIS MATCH – The Mating Game, Life –Relationships.

FOREIGN COUNTRY (If larger than your own) – A need to expand your awareness.

FRANCE – Sexual liberation.

FRONT DOOR or HALL -Vagina, birth canal.

FRONT GARDEN- Facing life or how we perceive the future.

GARAGE – Healing of the body.

GERMANY – Arrogance, regimentation.

GRAVE or TOMB – The stomach (storage of dead meat).

GREEN FIELDS – Healing, harmony, etc. (See 'Colors'.)

HAIRDRESSER – Change the way you think.

HOLIDAY SCENE – Need relaxation. Choice of 'next holiday' – Next life?

HOME (room not specified) – How your state of mind was influenced by your family.

GOING 'HOME" – Your Life Purpose or possibility of passing over.

HOMETOWN – Influences from the past, birth.

HOSPITAL or SURGERY – How your state of mind influences your health or healing.

HOT COUNTRY – A need for passion or emotion in your life.

HOTEL – Reception of your birth, healing the affect of birth.

IN COMPANY OF PARTNER / SIGNIFICANT OTHER – Nature or pattern of your relationships and/or healing for such.

JEWELRY SHOP – Spiritual values.

JOURNEY by boat -The dreamer's spiritual life. What you take "on board" or pick up from others. Birth esp. if boat is" berthed".

KITCHEN – Digestion, facing the day, rebirthing.

LIBRARY – Your inner wisdom, knowledge.

MOVING DOWNWARDS – Accept your physical / emotional aspects, birth or practical application of an idea, To the LEFT – Female aspect, emotion or past: To the RIGHT – Male aspect, intellect.

ROAD – Circulatory system, veins and arteries.

NARROW ROAD – a narrow state of consciousness, minor veins or arteries

controlling attitude.

OLD WORLD setting (as in castle, cobblestone courtyard, period costumes, etc.) – Past life influences.

OPERA – Need to express emotions.

POST OFFICE – Spirit medium, channeling.

PRISON or former Soviet country – Repressionof expression.

PUB – Social contact, blotting out sensitivity / emotion.

RAILWAY STATION- Birth.

ROAD running PARALLEL to a RIVER – Your spiritual path, philosophy of life.

SCHOOL – Learning about yourself with a view to improving yourself – The Halls of Learning in Spirit.

SEASIDE – Your approach to spirituality or life.

SHOP or SUPERMARKET – What you actually need, think you need, your accountability, digestion.

SLAUGHTERHOUSE – Self destruction.

THEATRE – on stage – Performance anxiety. In the audience -Looking at life.

TOILET – need to eliminate negative ideas or emotions, the elimination system.

JUNCTION especially T JUNCTION- Choices ahead – Y JUNCTION – Karma or Dharma.

TRACK, 'dirt or train track' –Digestive tract.

TRAIN CRASH – Possible problems with digestive system.

UNIVERSITY – The gift of wisdom, higher knowledge.

UPSTAIRS – Mental, spiritual aspects.

USA – A need for independence, energy, new ideas.

WEDDING – Uniting your male / female aspects, marriage or partnerships need healing, your suitability for a partnership.

WORKPLACE –working on yourself

When you have established the subject matter of the dream by considering the location – everything that appears there may be relevant to how the dream is trying to:

(A) HEAL YOU,

(B) GIVE YOU GUIDANCE, OR

(C) ALLOW YOUR SHADOW SELF TO OBJECT TO THE CHANGES OFFERED

If the dream moves to another location,

the subject matter may also have changed.

OTHER SYMBOLS

ACCIDENT- what you are doing to yourself

AEROPLANE- hope, new venture, plane crash= depression.

ANIMAL- Natural instincts.

ALARM(burglar, fire, alarm) – immune system

ARTICULATED, COMMERCIAL TRUCK – Male (cab) and Female (container) aspects needed in business venture.

BABY – Life Purpose.

BAGGAGE – Issues, usually from former life.

BAND OR ORCHESTRA – glands

BED – Sexuality, Reproductive System.

BIRDS (positive) – Ideals,

BICYCLE – Physical body, Exercise esp. for Circ. System. Tai Chi (balance of yin/yang)

BUS – Mothering, leadership, mother's body, birth.

BOOK, film or play – Life Purpose.

BUILDING (parts of) – Physical functioning or parts of the body.

CARPET, floor – understanding.

CAR – Physical body.

CASTLE – Former life,over-protectiveness.

CAT – Instincts, intuition.

CENTRAL HEATING – Circulatory System.

CIGARETTE – Cancer risk – burning resentment.

CLOCK – Heart.

CLOTHES, chairs – Attitudes.

COAL – Repressed emotion (anger).

COMPUTER – Brain.

CRYSTALS, diamonds – Ability to use crystals, stones for healing or divining

CYLINDRICAL Objects – Channeling.

DANCING – Harmonizing glands. – Man and woman dancing = harmonizing male and female aspects and glands.

DOG – Love, immune system esp. if guard dog.

DOORS, gates – New chapter in your life.

DRESS- Femininity.

DRIVER (bus, train) – Leadership,

DRIVER (taxi) – One to one counselling.

DUCK – Glands – pun for 'duct'.

EARRINGS – Clairaudience.

EGGS or henhouse – Ovaries.

ELEVATOR, room, – esp. box room, hallway, kiosk – womb.

EXAMS, graduation, interview, custom or border official asking questions – spiritual progress

FEMALE – emotion or female aspect (positive or blonde) – positive emotion to develop our acceptance of femininity, (negative or dark) – negative emotion, (young) – renewed emotion (very old) – former life emotional pattern, (ill or deformed) – state of your female aspect.

FINGER NAILS – natural instincts,

FIREPLACE – Heart.

FISH – Spiritual life.

FLOWERS – Love.

FOOTWEAR – ability to make progress, relationship.

FRIDGE – stomach

FROG – glands.

GLASS in window – your outlook or insight.

GLASS (broken) – risk of arthritis.

GRASS – blood.

HAIR – thought pattern.

HANDBAG – femininity.

HEDGE, Hedgehog – over-protection.

HORSE- healing.

HORSE AND CART –Healing (with male and female aspects).

JEWELS – spiritual gifts

KEY – power, responsibility, maturity.

LAMP, light – awareness

MALE- intellect or idea, male aspect, (positive or blonde) – positive aspect to develop or acceptance of your maleness. (negative) – effect of Dad or your opinion ofall men, (young) –new idea (very old) – former life pattern of thought, (ill or deformed) – state of male aspect.

MUSICAL instrument – channeling.

MONEY – energy, healing, commitment orinvestment in project, poverty consciousness, etc.

MOUSE – fear,

NUN – old style spirituality

OVEN – womb.

PEARL necklace – speaking wisdom.

PHONE – telepathy, family ties.

PHOTO – objective image of you.

PHOTOCOPIER – Reproductive System.

PIPES – veins, arteries, channeling.

PICTURES (art) – ideals.

PLASTIC – inorganic chemicals in body.

PLUMBING – waterworks of body.

POLICEMAN – application of Karmic Law.

POLICEWOMAN – Dharma.

PRESIDENT, politician – leadership potential.

PRIEST – former life, old stylespirituality.

RATS, sharks, foxes, man-eating tigers, worms, cannibals, etc. – cancer risk.

RODS, poles – male aspect.

ROYALTY – spiritual leadership potential.

ROPE or chain –Ties that Bind procedure (see Ch. 20)

STAIRS, steps – spine and/or raising your consciousness (see Ch. 20)

SALT – bitterness.

STATUE – cold, aloof emotionally unexpressive.

SUIT – conformity.

TEAPOT – heart.

TEETH – ability to cope with instincts e.g. childbearing oraggression.

TELEVISION – clairvoyance.

TREE – maturity, family tree, genetic inheritance.

VAN or commercial vehicle – work issues.

WASHING machine – stomach.

WALKING – exercise.

WALL – heart wall – emotionally overly protective of the self.

WINDOW – view of life.

WINDOW SILL – glands.

WINDOW left open – issue with immune system?

WING mirrors of car – testicles.

Remember, when you write out your dream, list the above symbols under the headings, "I am. I need or I can be" in relation to the subject matter. If the symbol you are looking for is not listed above, simply focus your mind on it; relax (follow the instructions in chapter 6), and ask the object:

"WHAT ARE YOU?

WHAT DO YOU DO?

WHAT ASPECT OF ME DO YOU REPRESENT?"

LEARN TO TRUST WHAT ANSWER COMES

17

CHAKRAS, CHAKRA HEALING AND COLORS

In our dreams, color is divided into three categories; healing colors, colors that give guidance, and the dark colors of our Shadow Self. Bright shades and positive combinations – colors plus white – are a form of healing and guidance. Red, e.g. can be very energizing while blue is more calming. The darker shades and combinations – colors plus black – are a reflection of personal fears and reservations about such healing and guidance. These darker shades can also be health warnings. So, how does this work and why do we dream of color?

To remain healthy the physical body requires a sufficient and balanced supply of energy. This comes mainly from food and drink but in common with the flowers and trees we also draw energy from the sun. This comes as white light which is transformed into different colored energies by a series of transformers called chakras.

THE CHAKRAS

There are 7 major chakras situated in a straight line along your spinal column. These are energized by the 7 primary colors which you see in the rainbow – red, orange, yellow, green, blue, indigo and violet. Each chakra dispenses the appropriate colored energy required by the organs, glands and systems in the immediate vicinity of that chakra. The remaining energy left over after this process seeps out through the skin and forms into an egg-shaped energy field around the body called the aura.

The three lower chakras including red at the base of the spine, orange at the sacral vertebra and yellow at the solar plexus are concerned with basic instincts – survival, sexuality and career respectively while the three upper chakras including blue at the throat, indigo at the brow and violet at the top of the head are concerned with higher considerations –

philosophy of life, psychic perception and spiritual purpose respectively. The heart chakra, in the middle exerts a balancing effect and is mainly concerned with emotional sharing. Negative thinking in relation to any one of these considerations over a period of time can damage the chakra involved and make it less effective. This, in turn can make you ill. So, if any of the primary colours frequently appear in your dreams-whether in a clear or darkened shade it can be a warning of impending trouble in the area influenced by the corresponding chakra.

COLOUR HEALING IN YOUR DREAMS

Your dreams will try to correct any irregularity in the energy by introducing the required color even if the remaining part of the dream is in monochrome. Positive shades or pleasant, beautiful combination of colours can be listed under "I need" while negative shades, negative combinations or limitation of the color by reducing it to stripes or checkering are listed under "I am". All colours in dreams have healing qualities with the exception of black and grey. The three lower colors – red, orange and yellow are stimulants while the three upper colors – blue, indigo and violet are coolants. Green brings a balance.

WHITE

In dreams this is the symbol of enlightenment, confidence, perfection, faith, hope and purity. When white is associated or mixed with the primary colors it purifies and refines their meaning. For example blue = your philosophy of life. A light blue – blue + white could indicate the need for a lighter or more enlightened spiritual outlook. White alone can indicate a rigid, proud, judgmental immaturity – a 'should-be' perfectionist with a controlling attitude.

BLACK

This represents negativity e.g. fear, depression (no hope), suspicion etc. When mixed with the primary colors it limits their purpose. For example red = passion, so if that color appears with black it can mean hatred. Black represents the Shadow Self which is in all of us.

BLACK AND WHITE

This represents immature, simplistic extremism – a 'black and white', judgmental or intolerant person.

– "if something isn't good it must be bad." This can cause trouble especially in relationships where the other party will be judged with impossibly high standards. Naturally, if you often dream of this combination you will be constantly angry, frustrated and stressed until you learn that people including yourself are not perfect. Look out for dreams of playing football (relationships – the 'mating game' or the 'game of life') especially with a black and white ball. Other competitive games can also indicate the pattern of your relationships.

GREY

Grey is a mix of black with white and usually means the denial or repression of emotion or lack of commitment.

RED

This primary color represents joy, passion, love, survival, courage, aggression and sexuality as a basic, animal or survival instinct. It can also appear in dreams to heal birth and gender issues, anxiety, allergies, etc. It can re-energize and heal the base chakra and its associated area of influence e.g. to nourish the blood, lower reproductive organs (testicles, vagina) bladder, legs and feet. In relationship dreams it usually indicates what is lacking in your love life. Here's an example; A young man about to be married dreamt that he was looking at his fiancé through a square hole in the wall of her bedroom. She was trying on her wedding dress which, to his surprise was grey with a borderline of red. A male colleague from the bank where he works appears and says; "I know how much money she has." The limited amount of red indicates a lack of passion and 'border-line' sexuality. The color grey indicates a lack of commitment or emotion. He is more concerned about financial considerations. Coarser shades of red such as scarlet can indicate lust while pink (mix of red and white) usually means compassion or mother love.

ORANGE

This color also refers to sexuality but of a more adult, committed variety. Negative thinking such as guilt or conflict over sexuality, intimacy, acceptance of self and others, embracing new ideas, etc. can darken the shade and may indicate a health warning. Orange energy feeds the 2nd. chakra at the sacral vertebra. This color heals and nourishes the upper reproductive organs (uterus, ovaries and prostate gland), lower back, colon, kidneys, etc. Consider the following dream from an elderly man; "I was walking in my back garden (the colon). When I came to the water feature (bladder) I found a dead rat beside a half-peeled disheveled – looking orange fruit (2nd. chakra)." The dream represents the danger of prostate cancer. Cancer cells (the dead rat) are being produced here but the immune system is killing them.

SAND COLOR, BEIGE, BLONDE OR CREAM

When white is mixed with the primary color orange it produces these colors which invariably means that the dreamer needs to develop acceptance, tolerance and maturity- e.g. a blonde woman = need to accept femininity.

BROWN

When black is mixed with orange it produces brown which means earthiness. Dark brown = Too earthy, the denial of spirituality and depression.

YELLOW

This primary color in a dream stimulates the intellect, will power, and self confidence. It helps us to rationalize and come to terms with fear especially about 'growing up', career, money issues and individuality. It can also be used to heal the 3rd chakra and in particular, the stomach (digestion), liver (arthritis, skin) small intestines, gall bladder, pancreas, (diabetes), adrenals, kidneys, etc. To help you eliminate habitual negative emotions, obsolete, childish habits or unhelpful people your dreams may put you with symbols representing these in a toilet sometimes decorated in yellow.

BRIGHT YELLOW

When white is mixed with yellow the bright yellow it produces indicates an enlightened or intuitive intellect.

NEGATIVE SHADES OF YELLOW

When black is mixed with yellow the resultant mustard shade indicates the inability to rationalize – hence the term "yellow" meaning cowardice or inability to rationalize whatever concerns you. Consider the following re-birthing dream from a lady in my dream group; "I was in a small mustard colored room (the womb). I was terrified of the men who waited for me outside (picking up mother's fears and issues with men). I was greatly relieved to hear workmen (Healing Agents) coming to repaint the room a brighter shade of yellow."

GREEN

This color appears in dreams to heal conflict over openness, harmony, trust, sharing, giving and receiving love, mothering (breast and lung ailments including cancer), self-protection, grief, denial, etc. It is also concerned with the balance of energy in your body and how that may affect your heart e.g. by too much eating and not enough exercise, too much work and not enough play, too much intellect and not enough emotion, etc. This primary color feeds the 4th chakra and nourishes the heart, immune system, lungs, breathing, blood pressure, lymph glands, arms, hands etc. Look for dreams about the state of grass. This can indicate the possibility of issues with the blood. Instead of a lush green lawn you might see patches of mud (pollution from the colon), broken glass (crystalline deposits of arthritis) or soggy wet paper mixed (mucus).

DREAM

Consider the following dream from a 48 year old man which was one of many warning him about possible cardiac problems; "I was working in a petrol filling station on Dublin's north quays. The traffic here is one way but in the dream it was a two way flow. One stream of traffic was heavier than the other. I was expected to work with my wife and my first duty was to mow the grass margin between the two lanes of traffic."

INTERPRETATION

See the petrol pump as his heart – sharing its energy with others. Working with the emotional, feminine aspect of himself (his wife in the dream) can also heal his heart. The imbalance in the flow of traffic = imbalance of his energy.

Black or grey mixing with the green producing negative, darker shades such as bottle green, or battle dress green can also spell trouble.

BLUE

Blue can symbolize our philosophy of life. This includes religion, art, culture, spiritual expression or anything we regard as sacred. If mixed with white the result is a lighter shade of blue meaning enlightened spirituality – which should be listed under 'I need'. If the healing agent in your dream is wearing light blue or blue and white or you are in a room decorated with these colors, you are being guided towards a more aware philosophy of life. This is a form of healing. Darker shades of blue (blue/black) indicate a negative philosophy of life such as an understanding of religion based on fear or the belief that life is 'a valley of tears'. These darker shades can also refer to trouble brewing in the throat chakra usually due to not expressing how you feel and/or not forgiving yourself or others, an excessive sense of guilt in other words, not listening to others and being judgmental. This primary color feeds the 5th. chakra situated at the throat and nourishes the throat, thyroid, parathyroid, neck, esophagus, ears (not listening to others), sinus, shoulders, arms and hands, etc. This color can also help you fight infections, colds, flu, etc.

Dark blue can also refer to the residual emotions of former lives in religious institutions. A nun of my acquaintance who entered the convent because of her (sub-conscious) fear of life had a dream where she was running, terrified, deeper and deeper into the convent building. She eventually came to a room where she found a couch draped in blue and white. The couch, being a cozy and relaxing piece of furniture, was a form of healing asking her to relax, meditate and assume an easier attitude to life. The healing color is white – to give her confidence – in relation to her philosophy. A bright shade of blue does not indicate that the dreamer has a positive philosophy of life but rather that he or she needs to develop such an attitude. Blue also has a calming, cooling, effect and is often used to relax and soothe people of an excitable or nervous disposition. Darker or "polluted" shades of color (blue and black) indicate the presence of fear or other negative emotions blocking the healing or guidance.

INDIGO

This color helps you to resolve spiritual or mental conflict often due to refusal to use your gift of clairvoyance, clairaudience seeing the future, etc. It can appear if you are having problems with the 6th chakra situated at the brow affecting the Autonomic Nervous System, mental peace, brain issues (migraine, strokes, tumors, motor skills, M.S., M.E., Motor neuron disease, Parkinson's, memory problems, Alzheimer's, etc. issues with pituitary gland, eyes, ears, deafness, (not listening to 'Holy Orders' coming from the Higher Self/ Real You.)

VIOLET

This primary color energizes the 7th chakra at the crown of the head and influences the pineal gland, head, hair, brain and Central Nervous system. It helps you to let go past life issues and conflict with your Life Purpose, the use of absent healing, telepathy and spiritual love. It can have a calming effect and heal parts of the brain, headaches and sleep problems arising from these mental conflicts. This chakra is the point at which, as a spirit we enter the body and finally leave it at death so the feeling of calm, peaceful acceptance which the color violet can bring can aid these transitions.

OTHER SPIRITUAL COLOURS

GOLD

Energy or hands-on healing

SILVER

Intuition

SOFT OR PEARLY WHITE

Wisdom

PURPLE

Spiritual leadership, spiritual teaching (Bishops wear purple)

GREEN AND PEACH

Counselling skill (Green helps to balance or

harmonize conflicting parties and peach indicates empathy. Both are good qualities in a counsellor)

To better understand the use of color in dreams, check the following:

(1) The combination, shade and state (e.g. dark shades, color combined with black, color described as "striped or checkered" may suggest how you subconsciously limit the color healing).

(2) Who is wearing or bringing positive colors? A Guide or healing agent doing so may suggest that they are what you need in life.

(3) Where the colors appear in relation to the dreamer – e.g. directly in front, up in the air, or above eye level -something to reach or strive after. Colors seen underfoot or below eye level may indicate emotions considered 'beneath you' or unworthy of your consideration especially if they are dark or negative. For example, black and white tiles on the floor = extremism. Yellow day-old chicks in the toilet = immature fears.

FOUR TYPES OF DEPRESSION

Dark brown (denial of spirituality)

Grey (denial of emotion)

Dark blue: ('oppressive' type of spirituality)

Black (feeling there is no hope)

FOUR TYPES OF POLLUTION IN THE BLOOD

(if the following appear with water or grass)

Brown: (pollution from the colon).

White: (mucus).

Plastic: (inorganic chemicals).

Broken glass: (arthritis)

Is the color being used to (a) heal, (b) enlighten, (c) as an expression of sub-conscious negativity or (d) warning of problems brewing in the relevant chakra and its area of influence?

COLOURS AND HEALING POWER

Consider these points in relation to what we know of color so far. Take red, the color of animal passion, fun, love, sex, etc. Animal passion includes aggression, which sometimes turns to anger, but we may need that aggression, that willingness to continue the struggle for life if our energy is low.

White, on the other hand, is hope, confidence, enlightenment, etc. The healing power of a combination of red and white in the same dream is clear.

DREAM

A woman whose 21 year old son was tragically killed in a fall from a cliff had the following dream: 'I saw my son standing in the prow of a sailing ship. It had a brilliant white sail with a red Crusader cross on it and was moving at full speed before a strong wind. Land was in sight'.

INTERPRETATION

Her son, in this dream, plays a positive role so he acts as the Healing Agent. The colors he brings are white for hope and confidence, and red for joy, energy, courage. The dream is designed to reassure her that despite her son's tragic death he is O.K. and on course to find his place in Spirit.

HOW COLOURS SHOW UP IN DREAMS

Orange helps us with digestion and elimination problems which go hand in hand with career difficulties as any ulcerated businessman will tell you. Orange energizes and when it combines with yellow and appears in dreams about career it helps you to pursue your ambition with confidence. The yellow can help work related stress and the assimilation of food.

Brown is the color of practicality. It heals in dreams by helping to earth people who are too much 'up in the air', in other words, those who have difficulty putting ideas to practical use. These are people who, being of an overly spiritual or other-worldly nature have difficulty adjusting to the nitty-gritty of everyday life on the Earth plane. They can also be healed by dreaming of pleasant shades of brown or more usually combinations of brown (earth), and green (reconciliation). Some people unfortunately go the opposite way and become too practical or too materialistic at the expense of their spirituality. Their dreams show dull or dark shades of brown as the sub-conscious expression (Shadow Self).

As a spirit functioning on the earth plane all of us require some form of spiritual expression and if we limit this to any great extent we can expect to suffer from depression as these negative shades of brown suggest. Dark brown (brown and black mix) means we are clinging to materialism out of fear (black) and the absence of faith and hope (white) will naturally bring our spirits down. Dull brown or brown minus the white of enlightenment can indicate an unenlightened practicality or materiality out of ignorance of any other goal.

DREAM

A woman dreamt that she met her father at the airport. He was wearing a dull brown jacket and grey trousers. Upon seeing her he turned his back and, without a word, walked up a flight of stairs. She followed him.

INTERPRETATION

This is another rebirthing dream and shows the on-going effect of the dreamer's father apparently rejecting her (turning his back) when she was born. The colors he wears indicate her reaction to that first meeting.

When a parent, partner or indeed anyone playing a negative role, appears in a dull, unpleasant, dark, or tarnished shade or combination of colors, it indicates that we have copied or 'picked up' negativity. 'Climbing up' as in the above dream is aspiring towards an ideal. Following in Dad's footsteps up the flight of stairs is an indication that she accepted his ideals. So, what were those ideals and why were they so wrong for her? Colors generally reflect emotions. Grey is a non-color and like black it has no redeeming features. It indicates the denial of emotion. So, her father's dull or unenlightened earthiness (dull brown) and lack of emotional commitment were accepted by her as a role model. With such a psychological inheritance this woman found it difficult to be happy in a relationship and in trying to emulate her father she denied her own femininity by adapting a mainly masculine outlook on life. As a result of this she separated from her husband, suffers from sporadic bouts of depression, and underwent a hysterectomy.

If a female rejects her femininity the results can be disastrous. The reproductive organs can suffer as the awesome power of the sub-conscious mind is used in a self-destructive fashion. This is usually a result of her father's initial disappointment at the gender of his offspring. To counteract this, male healing agents will appear in her dreams wearing pleasant shades of brown, beige or cream (acceptance and tolerance) and red (healing for her sexuality / reproductive organs. If any of these colors appear to those who normally dream of white alone, they are being used to dilute the rigid intolerance suggested by the latter. They will have a softening effect on the immature perfectionism of white. This is common in the dreams of teenagers especially when the delicate subject of personal relationships is in focus.

Blonde hair might be described as cream colored and as a symbol of acceptance. If, in your dreams, a blonde haired woman wants to get intimate with you, even if you are of the same sex, you may be sure that she is a Healing Agent whose mission is to bring you a feeling of self-acceptance and tolerance. If you need to dream of this color it is usually because mother failed to share those qualities with you at the time of your birth. This would be further confirmed if the blonde woman was also wearing pink – an effort to heal you with acceptance and love. How you react to this therapy is a good indication of how willing or otherwise, you are to accept these finer qualities in yourself. Tolerance is essential for the harmony of personal relationships. If the Healing Agent is blonde, and/or wearing light shades of brown, this calls for a more pragmatic approach to matters of the heart and to life in general. The Healing Agent will appear as male or female depending on what quality you need to develop in relation to the subject matter.

Further techniques for healing and balancing the chakra system can be found in the e-book.

Before we leave the subject of color healing in dreams and chakras one might reasonably ask; how do colors heal and make us feel better? Why, e.g. does red excite or encourage us or blue calm, soothe or relieve pain? This is not entirely psychological. Scientific studies in Norway e.g. have found that people in rooms or houses painted blue set a thermostat three degrees higher than those whose premises are decorated in red. This applies also to blind people who obviously cannot see the colors.

THE 7 STEPS TO AWARENESS

The early Christians seem to have known about the 7 chakras and, being healers they initiated a series of 7 techniques which can have a healing effect on the chakra system. These came to be known as the 7 sacraments; - (1) Baptism (2) Eucharist, (3) Confirmation, (4) Matrimony, (5) Confession, (6) Holy Orders and (7) Last Rites. Baptism seems to have been designed to spiritually cleanse the incoming spirit by the(removal of entities and negative energy and help it to feel connected to the Earth and the tribe. Indeed, the ritual still involves invoking the child to "renounce the Devil". Like the

1st chakra, the energy of all this seems to provide a foundation for growth and development. The Eucharist ritual includes eating bread and drinking wine which, taken at its face value suggests or brings about an enhanced enjoyment of life. In the process this could help the 2nd chakra.

Confirmation is a puberty ritual and as such it is consistent with the energy of the 3rd chakra which is about accepting the responsibility of adulthood. Matrimony, like the 4th chakra ideally unites the male and female energies in a sharing of love. Confession, like the energy of the 5th chakra encourages the expression and release of guilt. The ritual of 'Holy Orders' involves commitment to spiritual service which is similar to the 6th chakra ethic. Finally, the last Rites and the 7th chakra prepare the soul for its final exit from the body. Is it a coincidence that these early Christians also came up with 7 "deadly" sins; – Pride, Covetousness, Lust, Anger, Gluttony, Envy and Sloth? These are not sins in the sense of bad actions but negative states ofconsciousness which would cause one to live in conflict with the positive ethics of the chakras, create illness and retard spiritual development.

THE SEVEN AGES OF MAN

The 7 sacraments seemed to have been a series of rituals which were also designed to heal the 7 ages of man.

These are:

(1) Birth and early childhood up to the age of 7 including the child's first impressions of the self and the World.

(2) The age of Reason 7 – 11/12 years during which a more rational understanding of life can be formed.

(3) Puberty and the teens to age 20 – a time of confusion and painfully learning to come of age but also an opportunity to assert one's individuality. (4) Young adulthood 21 – 50 – building responsibility through creating a family, trade or status.

(5) Mid-life crisis and re-appraisal or life 51 – 60.

(6) Exploration of one's spirituality or philosophy of life. This raises the question; "What else is there to life?"

(7) Letting go, legacy and passing on.

In each of the 7 ages above, an opportunity is

presented to re-invent the self. Dreams will have a lot to say about what choices are made. These passages from one stage of development to another are usually depicted as doorways.

18

THE MEANING AND USE OF NUMBERS

Numbers like everything else in dreams can be divided into "I am", "I need" and "I can be". They tend to be male (straight lines) and female (curved lines). The male aspect (yang) in life is inclined to make us more rigid, artificial and limiting while the female (yin) can be more spontaneous, intuitive and free flowing. The male can appear as 1 and the female can be indicated as 0. The interaction of these male and female aspects of the self represents the upward journey of the soul to awareness and re-unification with the Source.

0

Zero a circle having no beginning or end can be seen as God – the Divine Female, ideals or goals. A sphere can have the same meaning. The figure 1 (male) represents individuality and self assertion. Establish your identity, break free from the herd and begin your individual quest. The journey ends with the 1 and 0 coming together to produce 10 – alignment with God or the Real Self. The extent to which you achieve this or are experiencing it in present time can bring a measure of health, wealth, happiness, success and good 'luck'. This is your natural state in this life and spiritual development of the soul. So, numbers ask you to decide who and what you are and who and what you choose to be. They can also indicate a memory from the age of a child appearing in the dream.

1

I represents the need to know yourself – esp. the faults and weaknesses of your Shadow Self – only then can you plot your journey to 10 – completion of your quest.

2

2 usually indicates the pattern of your relationships

e.g. "two uncomfortable, ill-matched shoes", "cat and dog." two "love birds" and so on. 2 can also suggest channeling – the ability to function in two dimensions but also being indecisive – "of two minds".

3

3 is commitment. – giving of yourself in body, mind and spirit to e.g. a cause, relationship or project. List it under "I need "or "I can be" in relation to the subject matter. 3 is also a 'magic 'number with a power of its own. The triangle or three-sided pyramid would have the same meaning. Napoleon Hill, a motivator and therapist to Henry Ford the car manufacturer and Thomas Edison the inventor called this the 'Power of Three'. Three people would meet to meditate in a small cabin owned by Ford. They would come up with new ideas to make them even wealthier. Phyllis Krystal used a 3 sided Triangle of Light in the process of 'Cutting the Ties that Bind'. This can focus the mind and heart to God or Higher Consciousness. The sub-conscious understands this symbol and responds with co-operation.

4

4 = the artificial limitations you put on aspects of yourself. A square, rectangle or box would have the same meaning e.g. "flowers in a box" = limited or artificial love.

5

5 = Karma .The numbers 5 and 6 relate to each other – Karma is the harsh, male application of the Laws of Attraction and Cause and Effect i.e. awareness through suffering.

6

6 = Dharma – the more merciful female application of these Laws using a path through forgiveness, love and spiritual service. For example; you might dream that you are expected to pay a bill (the debt you owe or think you owe from former life misdeeds) and you are given a choice as to how to pay – e.g. £50 or $60. In appearance, 5 and 6 seem similar in having a semi-circular or circular base – representing the cycle of life, death and rebirth with lines (straight or male as in 5 and curved, female as in 6.) These represent a choice of ways to evolve and escape from the need to reincarnate on Earth.

7

7 = Spiritual awareness. 7and 9 also relate to each other – again as male and female while 8 in between can balance them out. 7 = the limit of awareness the male aspect can help you to achieve through the intellect, books or conventional wisdom. It consists of a straight line ascending to another straight level line (the highest male level of awareness). In dreams it usually means "you know better than the way you are behaving".

8

8 = the balance between the male and female. When you list this under "I need" you will realize how your life is out of balance. For example you may be taking life too seriously and stressing yourself out, too much work and not enough fun, or otherwise in need of moderation – in which case your might dream of 48 (limited balance). Phyllis Krystal uses the figure '8' in meditation to help people separate psychologically from the negative influence of parents and establish their own identities. The two circles involved can help people to set their own boundaries (separate ideals).

9

9 = the height of awareness the female aspect can take you through love, forgiveness, intuition, etc. It consists of a straight line ascending to a circle (God aspect.) 9 can also mean the completion of a cycle of lives in which you were trying to learn a positive quality. Look for "nine terraced houses"in a dream. In the best case scenario it might mean your last life on Earth. In which case "Congratulations"!

DREAMS

Consider the following dreams. Both dreamers were male and involve numbers and puns. Puns are important in dreams and usually contain the essence of the dream.

(1)

'I took my wife shopping for shoes. The owner of the shop insisted that she try on a pair in his garden which was full of beautiful flowers. The shoes were oddly different and did not seem to match. I asked him how much? He replied "36". I did not want to spend too much on her. I was surprised to see an elderly priest from the seminary where I was educated leave the shop.'

(2)

'I found myself, accompanied by a little dog entering a huge department store. I went into an elevator and I knew my job was to deliver magazines to people on different levels of the building. I would go up to the 7th floor and then come down to the various floors to make deliveries. At one point the elevator went up through the roof of the building and flew through the air. I could hear a voice telling me not to be afraid'.

MY INTERPRETATIONS

(1)

This dream attempts to bring happiness into the life of the dreamer who is in an incompatible relationship (two oddly matched shoes). The Guide (shop keeper) asks him to improve the relationship with openness (the garden) commitment (3 and money) and love (6 and flowers). The dreamer was a priest in a former life. (36 is a pun for 'dirty sex)'.

(2)

This dreamer was born (going into elevator in large building) to be a channel and deliver information (magazines) which she can access from her spiritual knowledge (7) and bring to others on various levels of awareness. However, she is asked to do this with love (the dog) and with even higher knowledge from other dimensions (flying). Puns; "thinking outside the box" and "crashing through the glass ceiling" (artificial limitations to her potential).

19

THE 'PERSONALITY' OF ILLNESS

When Dreams deal with your issues, illness and apparent 'bad luck', they invariably show you that the cause is usually stress – created by your personality. So, the message of a dream is – if you want to change the future for the better you must change yourself. It is well known that certain personality types produce predictable illnesses and issues. To understand how this process works you have to accept that chronic illness is, to a great extent based on negative memories from birth, early childhood usually up so the age of 7 and former lives. The energies these memories produce tends to 'live' in various and symbolic parts of the body e.g.

sexual guilt in the prostate gland, grief in the heart and so on. The Law of Attraction (Cause and Effect) enables this process to work, like a mathematical formula. The cause will continue to create the effect until you eliminate it. This will apply to cancer and all other chronic illness. Men, especially if scientifically trained, tend to think that the cause must come from outside factors such as what we eat, drink, read or otherwise take into our bodies. Women, especially if intuitive, or aware, can more readily accept the incredible power of habitual thought to heal or make us ill.

Please remember, dreams are not diagnoses. If you are ill, consult a doctor. However, it can be to your advantage to know what part of your personality contributes to the creation and perpetuation of your ailment. The following is a 'rough 'guide to that.

ARTHRITIS AND BACK PROBLEMS

As a general rule (with some exceptions) problems with the upper part of the body (above the waist) e.g. the chest, heart, lungs, etc. are connected to your issues with Mum. Ailments below the waist are generally down to Dad. The lower part of your body literally holds up and supports the upper. This is Dad's job. He is expected to be the 'backbone of the family' but memories of him being weak, ill or "not there for you" can 'live' in your spine and eventually create illness there. Look for dreams taking place on a staircase esp. if males appear to be "unhelpful, turn their backs or obstruct". Such dreams might include damage to the structure of the stairs or handrail for e.g. defective steps (vertebrae problems). Young children can develop curvature of the spine if the parents are incompatible with each other or Dad leaves.

Arthritis esp. in the hips, knees or feet might also be linked to Dad. This is usually down to resentment (unexpressed anger) at his character or behavior. It has been scientifically proven that such feelings can chemically change the chemical composition of the blood and produce crystalline deposits of carbon which then lodge between the joints and produce arthritis. Look for dreams about rubbish in water (the blood) and esp. particles of broken glass appearing there or in the grass.

DIGESTION & ELIMINATION

This can be a judgmental, controlling, 'black and white' personality who is unable to 'go with the flow' of life. His or her dreams might suggest that fear (black) causing over-controlling of the self or others (white) can result in a slow-moving, toxic or hardened bowel. Parts of the colon can be squeezed or twisted from stress leaving other parts bulged. Food can remain there too long. Fermentation can occur and particles can seep out causing pollution of the blood. Dream examples; "A black and white cat tangled up in a pair of tights (the colon)" or "slugs slowly moving along a cement 'back passage' in the garden –(sluggish, hardened colon,) etc.

ALLERGIES

Dream (Female); "I was living in war-torn Berlin. My mother was an enemy agent who had booby-trapped all the food in the house. I was terrified to eat anything in case it might explode." Interpretation; Stress from memories of her mother in this and a former life they shared in Germany in World War 2 are causing an allergic reaction in present time. The dreamer may be a critical, judgmental type of personality.

LACTOSE INTOLERANCE

Dream; (young female); "I met a nice young man and took him home for coffee. Unfortunately my mother was at home and started asking him probing, searching questions. I was seething with anger and embarrassment. I noticed that the milk I was heating on the stove was boiling over and dropping onto the floor in a 'thick, white slime'. Interpretation; A pattern of anger at her mother from the time of her birth (mother's milk) can be turning milk and dairy produce into mucus ('white slime'). Mucus can also appear as snow, wet paper esp. in grass. Critical, judgmental type.

HEART AND CIRCULATORY SYSTEM

The heart personality tends to be emotionally reticent, overly protective of the self and builds up a psychological 'heart wall'. This inhibits the flow of energy and can produce cardiac issues. The wall is invisible at first but over a period of time it can solidify into an actual wall as mucus builds up in the chest area and sinuses. This can also contribute to blocked arteries. In dreams look out for clocks, teapots, car engines (heart), walls, hedges, suits of armor (over-protection), islands, apartments, detached houses (emotional isolation), banks, mention of one or two way streets, tea parties (need for emotional sharing), blocked roads, archways (pun for 'arteries'), cycling, walking, jogging (exercise). Stress esp. with work, family, relationships, etc. should be avoided. Stress, remember is not so much about what you do but rather how you feel about doing it.

BLOOD

The condition of water or grass in your dreams can refer to the state of your blood. Pollution can be indicated if the water is "full of rubbish or plastic", (inorganic chemicals from processed foods or medication). "a dirty brown color", (fecal waste from the colon) "slow moving"(circulation) and so on. If the grass is similarly described e.g. "brown patches in the lawn" (fecal waste), white material in the grass (mucus), "soggy, water-logged field (lymph glands) and so on. When Rule 2 is applied the above symbols can indicate the effect. The cause – the dreamer's state of mind will usually precede this in the dream. It will most likely end with or include some healing device. If not you can re-enter and change it by – perhaps draining the field, introduce a flowing river ('go with the flow of life') and so on.

BRAIN ISSUES, STROKES, MIGRAINE, ETC.

This can be a rigid, arrogant person conflicted or at war with the ideas and ideals of the Real Self. Look for two contesting opponents e.g. boxers hammering the heads of each other or falling headlong onto a concrete floor. Dreams of headstones (beliefs 'etched in stone') would also indicate the same mental rigidity. Such brain dreams might take place in an attic or refer to the ceiling, the top of a mountain, a computer or smart phone, the aisle of a church (two hemispheres of the brain.) and so on. Naturally, damage to any of the above would suggest possible injury or malfunction in the brain area in present or future time. For example; lightning striking the roof, water coming down through the ceiling, narrow roadways at the top of a mountain blocked or covered with snow (veins or arteries in the head area obstructed). The snow would suggest that a mucus/cholesterol producing diet should be avoided.

THE GLANDULAR SYSTEM

This works well when the energy of the body is balanced and harmonious. The glands, themselves are also male and female. They are situated throughout the body and they secret male and female hormones in response to instructions from the pituitary or master gland in the brain. This is not unlike musicians performing in an orchestra under the direction of the conductor and this is how it is often illustrated in dreams. The harmony or disharmony and the effect of this on your energy and health can also be indicated by a man and woman dancing e.g. Fred Astaire and Ginger Rogers from the old Hollywood musicals. Disharmony or imbalance between the male and female aspects of your body can cause confusion, discordant energy and illness. As a result e.g. in the reproductive system – the ovaries in the female and the prostate in the male may suffer. In the digestive system the thyroid gland or the thymus gland in the immune system could be affected and so on.

The glands can be over – active or under-active depending on the state of the male and female aspects of your energy. If the pancreas, which produces blood sugar is affected the result can be diabetes. Dreams will try to redress the deficiency. Consider this from a female dreamer: "I was walking along a footpath when I noticed honey or nectar seeping out of a wall and onto theground. I decided to put some of this into my lunchbox." Interpretation; The dreamer needs to believe that life can be sweet.

Another woman in a pre-diabetic state dreamt the following; "I was looking atan inside wall of a woman's house. I noticed that it was covered with holes. Some were stuffed with rags – others were secreting liquids. I started to remove the rags but my mother told me to put them back." Interpretation; Memories of poverty and deprivation (the rags) associated with femininity and motherhood are negatively affecting her glandular system.

The glands can also be indicated in dreams by the window sills of a house, frogs or ducks – presumably because they all appear to secrete liquid. 'Ducks' is a pun for 'ducts' – referring to their ability to conduct hormones.

Consider the following three dreams from a French man; (1) "I was an army officer during World War 1. I was full of manly courage and urged my men to advance against the enemy guns. They were slaughtered. A whole generation of young men was wasted in that war." (2) "I was shooting ducks" (3) "A young baby was causing great annoyance by constantly crying. I put two hand grenades inside hisdiapers' Interpretation; Sub – consciously he is creating negative energy in his reproduction system by repressed guilt and anger at his male aspect. Personality type – he would be inclined to be judgmental because of painful memories from childhood and former lives.

FERTILITY AND REPRODUCTIVE SYSTEM

It is obvious from the above dreams how the dreamer could develop problems with his testicles or prostate gland, This may be down to how welcome he felt at his birth. Would his parents have preferred a female child? Consider the following man's dream. His parents expected him to become a priest but instead he disappointed them by joining the police force. "I was taking my parents on a journey and even though we had been driving for hours we only arrived at Boyle, (pun for 'boy) a small town in the west of Ireland. I was anxious to conceal this from them. (Not 'gone far' or achieved enough in life) We met a policeman that I thought we knew but my father remarked "heis not the man I thought he was". I drove recklessly,crashing into bollards and damaging the wing mirrors. (Testicles)." I think the meaning is clear. Being judgmental about his manhood can damage his reproductive system. More usually such men have dreams about rods, rifles, screw drivers etc. being broken or malfunctioning.

Females with difficulties in this area tend to have dreams about containers described as "dirty, blocked or broken" etc. Examples "A man called to the door to repossess my oven (uterus –'bun in the oven').

I said; "Take it away. It's dirty. I never wanted it" Another woman dreamt that she met a man, took him home but in the morning he was gone leaving "scrambled eggs on the plate" (the affect of Dad on her ovaries)

It may seem unbelievable that people have the ability to create their own chronic ailments but, never underestimate the destructive power of the sub-conscious Shadow Self. Females coming especially from rural backgrounds where femininity is often unappreciated can suffer in this way. Young woman's dream; "I was back inthe farm where I lived as a child. The hen-house (egg production) was totally blocked with bird's droppings." It is important to understand how, as in this case a woman's ovulation can be blocked by pollution. Mucus, fecal matter and inorganic chemicals can be floating around in the blood. This can be difficult for the body to eliminate but if a woman has sub-consciously little respect for her femininity then two things can happen; (a) the pollution can be dumped into the uterus or ovaries and/or the immune system can be inhibited there.

Another woman who was sexually abused by a man as a child had eleven miscarriages. She related the following dream; "I was working in a gent's toilet cleaning a urinal with a wire scourer. I was rubbing the insideof it so hard the enamel lining was coming off" Interpretation; She felt used by men and was self-sabotaging her uterus.

CANCER

We are endlessly told that what we eat is very important and that is true, but when it comes to cancer, it might be more important to look at what is 'eating us'. People who have difficulty expressing anger, hurt, guilt and who internalise the stress and negative energy this causes can bring about illness. They tend to be critical, judgmental and condemn themselves. So it can be described as a form of self hate or self destruction. They are not consciously doing this. It is entirely the work of the sub-conscious Shadow Self.

Parts of the body and especially the cells have a consciousness. They communicate with each other. In the case of cancer they apparently decide one day to go on a rampage of self destruction. Why do they do this and why do they target specific parts of the body such as the womb, breast, prostate gland etc? If we have difficulty with some part of our functioning we can sub-consciously detach ourselves emotionally and energetically from that part. Starved of energy the immune system begins to fail there and we develop the illness. Look in dreams for negative life forms – criminals, rats, foxes, worms, wood worm, animals or fish esp. if mutated e.g. half cat and half rat or unnatural patterns of growth as in weeds, ivy or the roots or branches of trees. Smoking or leaving lighted cigarettes (burning anger) on a window sill (glands) can indicate the risk – even for non-smokers.

IMMUNE SYSTEM

Potential trouble with this can often appear as guard dogs esp. terriers trying to deal with rats (cancer cells), burglar alarms, smoke detectors, etc. If the guard dog appears to be exhausted then stress may be limiting your immunity. You may dream of windows being left open as burglars lurk outside or you may dream of people, especially doctors or nurses, who are unwilling to help you. Consider the following dream from a 45 year old female teacher: "All the alarms were going off in the school but everyone was ignoring them. Groups of teenagers were smoking in the corridors. I got out of the building and went upstairs in a bus. A window had been left open and a crow flew in. It burrowed into my chest and I could not get it out. I went to my brother but he refused to help saying that it probably laid its eggs inside me. Eventually, I went to a counselor friend who persuaded it to come out". Personality type; Critical, judgmental, self sabotaging, believing themselves to be unsupported or unprotected (influence of Dad) giving up on life, People, who develop a death wish, especially in old age, can retard their immune system.

If your issue or illness is not mentioned above use the '3M's technique described in Chapter 22 to bring to mind negative memories from your birth, early childhood or former lives which can help you understand how your personality may be connected to your problem.

20

PERSONALITY TYPES: ROLES PEOPLE PLAY

Power struggles and overly trying to control ourselves and other people are a common cause of disharmony and illness. We are all trying to control each other. You are trying to control your partner while he or she is trying to control you. Your parents tried to control you and you, from the earliest days tried to control them. We try to control each other by acting out familiar dramas or roles – like the child throwing a temper tantrum in the supermarket to influence her mother or 'falling off' her bike to get Dad's attention. Some children, who discovered that they get attention by being ill can sub-consciously get into the habit of creating illness in their bodies.

They may continue with this into adult life. An example is the child who, feeling powerless discovers that he can make his mother annoyed by refusing to co-operate with her attempts to toilet train him. This is called 'anal retention' and the habit can cause problems with his colon in later life.

Why do we do this? Oddly, enough we are all competing for energy. We engage in power struggles and the winner – the one who becomes the top dog 'draws 'energy from the other like a vampire. He or she feels good and the loser feels deflated. This becomes more obvious when you look at the relationship between a very dominant person and his or her partner. Habitually drawing energy from someone over a period of time can drain that person's immune system and make them physically ill, emotionally dependent or unable to think or make decisions. A wife might try to control her husband by constantly criticizing him or insisting that he phone her from work every day and so on. He, on the other hand might be trying to control her by playing the role of victim and, by playing 'hard done by' get her sympathy and in the process draw energy from her. It is an endless and unnecessary process which can cause havoc in relationships and health. To detect this in dreams ask the negative characters that appear; "What am I doing to myself because of you?"

In fact we create stress, trouble, illness and our eventual death by the negative aspects of our personalities which we call the Shadow Self. James Redfield in his book 'The Celestine Prophesies' identifies four habitual ways in which we try to control other people by acting out dramas. These are the Critic (or Interrogator), the Poor Me, the Intimidator and the Aloof. To avoid stress and illness in our lives it can be useful to know which Control Drama or combination of Control Dramas we use. Two are male and two female.

THE CRITICS: (MALE – ACTIVE)

These are the perfectionists. They constantly ask questions of themselves and others until they find the weaknesses they expect. They set impossibly high standards for themselves and others. They are overly responsible and will even take on the work of others. They tend to be critical, judgmental, snobbish and workaholic. Their reluctance to forgive and accept others can lead to resentment and arthritis or even cancer (judging and condemning themselves). This type can also be called the 'Judge'.

THE POOR ME'S: (FEMALE –PASSIVE)

These are the victims and constantly feel 'hard done by'. They sub-consciously seek out and invite people and events into their lives so that they, themselves end up poor, suffering or ill. They are emotionally immature and are often clinging, needy and dependent. Adult activities such as working 9 – 5, seven days a week or taking responsibility for themselves can be very stressful. They take redundancy at the first opportunity and perhaps go into business for themselves. This often fails due to their habit of 'thinking small' – or being 'penny wise and pound foolish'. Their need to suffer extends to health. When one illness is cured they create another to take its place. Some of these ailments can be unusual and may satisfy their need for attention and nurturing.

THE INTIMIDATORS: (MALE –ACTIVE)

They intimidate to win an argument. Their anger, arrogance, mental rigidity and stubbornness are the usual way by which they can be recognized. They always 'know best' and never express regret or gratitude. Being extremely competitive they will get stressed if there is any possibility of losing. They must have their 'own way' and control everything and everybody. This can cause trouble in relationships. They can be very mischievous and deliberately stir up trouble. They routinely manage to insult everyone. A good example of this is Donald Trump. They have a tendency to suffer brain issues in later life such as migraine, strokes, paranoia, obsessions, addictions, compulsions, insanity and eye problems. Margaret Thatcher for example, suffered a number of strokes – one of which eventually killed her. By obsessively trying to control others they can get stressed, bring on high blood pressure and/or a stroke. They must always have an enemy and if one is not there he must be invented as Hitler (another intimidator) did with the Jews. They never seem to learn – even from the hard lessons of experience.

THE ALOOFS: (FEMALE –PASSIVE)

They manipulate people by making themselves scarce and 'hard to get'. They are inclined to be independent, isolated – even within a family or group and like to keep people at a distance. They avoid emotional commitment or confrontation and tend to delay or procrastinate. They did not bond with mother at birth and consequently do not bond well with others. Marriage or committed relationships are like prison to them. When they are with one partner they are thinking about someone else. They do not live in the 'real world' but instead look out on life from 'ivory towers'. They act as if nothing is wrong – even when they are suffering and never say what they are really feeling. Their habitual illnesses are fear based and in the area of heart (building heart walls) and throat issues (not expressing anger). Variations include; 'Mister Nice Guy' and 'The Actor'. They make good counselors because of their objective view of life and it's problems. They tend to be emotionally or sexually repressed which does not endear them to partners and can lead to relationship issues.

NOTES ON CONTROL DRAMAS

The four Control Dramas are aspects of the Shadow Self which is driven by fear and obsessed with control. It apparently came to your aid when you were very young and felt totally out of control and at the mercy of others. It gave you a choice of four different ways to manipulate your parents and siblings by acting out dramas. Play-acting in this manner is based on the idea that if you cannot control others they control you and as a result you are in danger. This belief system became more and more real to you and continues into present time creating stress and illness. When, eventually you realize that they do not represent your Real Self you can release fear and 'open the door' to health, happiness, wealth, 'luck' and success.

21

STEPS TO AVOID CHRONIC AILMENTS

Cancer can be used to make a sub-conscious statement of martyrdom – usually to a parent. For example; "I will make myself ill. You will be sorry then for the way you treated me" This is more common in younger people and may appear in dreams as self destruction. These can include scenes of crucifixion, Jesus Christ, or someone making a statement in an extreme or extraordinary fashion. Consider the following dream from a woman in her late 30's who was diagnosed as being in the early stages of cervical cancer. "I was walking along the banks of the river which flows through the town where I live. The 'service entrance' to the shops is accessible from this area. I was horrified to find there a man and a woman who were horribly mutilated having been crucified. They were still alive but further up I found a dead man who had also been crucified."The dreamer had been given up for adoption at birth and sub-consciously she carried a death-wish program or martyr complex. The "service entrance" of the shops confirmed that cancer was being created in the cervix. 'Cutting the Ties' with her parents, forgiving them and herself for the adoption, re-entering and changing her dreams brought about a remission. That was some years ago and the cancer has not returned.

The self-defense mechanism responsible for fighting off disease is controlled by the sub-conscious. This part of the mind is super-efficient and will continue to support the physical body unless it receives orders to the contrary. Outside factors can have such an emotional impact that the sub-conscious turns to a self-destruct mode. The death of a husband is upsetting for most women but can be even more traumatic if it parallels the circumstances of her father's death. Particularly if the woman did not fully grieve, release and resolve the original event.

Resentment at being passed over for a promotion

in his job can cause a man to reactivate feelings of rejection by his parents. Infidelity in a marriage echoes injustice within the original family. All or any of these feelings can produce a death wish and the sub-conscious, in true computer fashion, responds to this new impetus by retarding the immune system. For most people, dreams are the only way of knowing what is going on in this area of the mind. A death wish appearing adds urgency to any health dream.

Dreams taking place in cemeteries or slaughter houses or in which you find yourself following someone who has died – especially of cancer, going through a series of doors, or terms are used such as 'crossing over to the other side of a road or river, leaving the cinema before the end of the movie, going home', etc. can indicate the death wish or program. This is like an escape clause that a young child can sub-consciously install especially if he or she feels unwanted or unloved.

The relationship a young child has with death can be difficult for an adult to understand. The newcomer, as a spirit has recently arrived from what might have been a better place to take up life in an unfamiliar animal body and in a strange, uncertain world. He or she can feel threatened and tries to make sense of what is happening. Children have greater access to long term memories. They can remember having lived and died before and can regard death as simply a door into another dimension. They search these archives to find parallel memories. Having the umbilical cord tighten around the neck while in the womb is obviously frightening but it would be even more so if one was hanged to death in a former life. Not being acceptable because of having a female body is frustrating but we would feel this even more intensely if, in a former life being female brought on suffering or death. In some cultures unwanted female children are killed. If a child feels that s/he has made a mistake by being born to a particular set of parents s/he is able to activate the self-destruct mechanism. This can easily be done within the first two years when his spirit is less attached to the physical body and, according to the Guides can result in what we call a 'cot death' as the child's spirit simply leaves the body. The death program or option can be put on hold and reactivated in later adult life. Such events as the death of a loved one, financial setbacks, marital breakdown, career problems, or any other experience about which the person feels deeply may be sufficient to push the button and begin the countdown to death. This can cause the immune system to break down and illness follows.

THE STEPS

(1) Obviously, you should avoid cigarettes, too much sun, take reasonable exercise and eat sensibly.

(2) Even more important than what you eat is what 'eats you'. Thinking badly about yourself or anyone else for more than 60 seconds can create negative energy. So, if you find yourself doing so repeat the mantra:"I love you. I'm happy. I thank you. I forgive and am forgiven" Indeed, we should all do this routinely several times a day.

(3) Scan your dreams. Look out for the 'usual suspects' to indicate cancer cells i.e. rats, sharks, foxes, worms, etc. plus any mention of the immune system – alarms, guard dogs, open windows, etc. Note any sign of the 'death wish'. Re-enter your dreams and change them as indicated.

(4) Be mindful of what stresses you. Learn to relax using the mantras and meditation system.

(5) Check out the state of your chakras – using Kinesiology (see Ch.21). If your dreams continuously

mention a specific color this may be a chakra in trouble.

(6) Consult your doctor if you have any reason to believe you are at risk.

(7) Study the Control Dramas and understand what aspect of your personality contributes to your issues or illness. For example, a combination of the Critic (self-hate by judging yourself) and the Aloof (suppressing the negative energy created by the Critic) can inhibit the immune system. The Poor Me can also create cancer cells by a desire to suffer or be a martyr. Try acting out of character. Stop judging and be kind to yourself.

(8) Keep your colon clean (exercise, fiber, fruit, etc.). Arguably, a slow-moving toxic bowel can be a breeding ground for this and other ailments. Hippocrates, the ancient father of medicine used to say;"Death (cancer?) lives in the colon and when the time comes it moves to it's final destination".

(9) A daily routine of meditation, mantras, physical exercise, tai chi (to balance the glandular system), and Cutting the Ties can be very helpful.

(10) If you have been diagnosed with having cancer

or a chronic illness, and are on medication the techniques outlined in this book can help and enhance the treatment. For example:

(a) Sending out a positive message to the Universe (and God) by repeatedly re-entering and changing any dream, even one not obviously referring to your illness. See yourself in the dream fully healed.

(b) Cosmically Ordering better Health as described in previous chapters.

22

HEALING TECHNIQUES

KINESIOLOGY

To fully understand dreams and healing it is important to remember that chronic illness is created by negative memories. These memories and their resultant belief systems exist in various parts of the body. They create negative energy there which can eventually make you ill. Knowledge and awareness is also stored in the body. Therapists take advantage of this and use the muscles to get "yes" and "no" answers to questions.

WAYS TO USE THIS TECHNIQUE

(a) Verify what your dreams are telling you. Symbols

can be interpreted in different ways. Check for "yes" or "no" if you are unsure what a symbol means.

(b) If you are using a mantra (as in Chapter 10) verify if it has been received or accepted by your brain. For example; "I'm happy. I accept myself" Check for "yes" and "no". If you get "no" repeat the mantra until you get "yes."

(c) When healing with the left and right hand (See Chapter 23 below) ask if enough negative energy has been extracted and then if enough positive infused. Continue with the healing until you get a "yes". Alternatively ask "have I extracted 10%, 20%, 30% negative energy from the affected area?

METHOD

(a) Stand with your back straight. Think of "yes" and allow your body to be swayed slightly backwards or forwards. Repeat by thinking of "no". Most likely, you will be swayed forward for "yes "and backward for "no".

Method (b) Link the tip of the thumb with the tip of the index finger of both hands making loops. Connect these together like a chain and try pulling them apart. When you think of "yes" and pull the link will be strong. It will be noticeably weaker for "no". Test your ability to get accurate answers with both methods using true and false statements. "My name is.........." (using a false name and then your true name). With practice, your answers will become more accurate. A word of caution – if you are asking questions about yourself or something about which you feel passionately you may be biased and your answers may be less accurate. When possible, ask an impartial friend to check for you.

T.A.R

All effective healing is based on a three-step process:

Trance, Awareness and Re-training (T.A.R.)

(1) Trance: Induce an altered state of consciousness in yourself or another e.g. with the 4 Minute Meditation or repeating a mantra. This can give you access to the computer-like sub-conscious mind.

(2) Awareness: Discover the cause of the issue or illness e.g. negative memory. What belief system has that memory given you about yourself or others? How does that limit you or make you ill in present time?

(3) Re-training: Teach your sub-conscious mind

(Shadow Self) to cleanse, erase or re-evaluate the memory. Re-train yourself to respond differently to people, things, events, etc.

You can apply the following techniques more effectively if you keep the above in mind.

MEMORY, MEANING AND MOVEMENT ('3M'S)

All dreams are based on memories and, as you know re-entering, understanding and changing them can be of great therapeutic benefit. If you cannot remember a dream, then doing the same to a memory can have a similar healing effect.

METHOD

In a journal, list exactly what you want to achieve – happiness, good relationships, money, healing for your cancer, heart, back, or whatever and write about how bad each item is in present time. Exactly how severe on a scale of 1 -10 is your depression? What is the pattern of your relationships, etc? This will make it clear to the Universe how you want your life to change and enable you to measure your progress (when you read this later).

Focus on one such issue or ailment each time you practice this.

[1]

MEMORY

Use the '4 Minute Meditation'(Chapter 4) or simply repeat several times the mantra: "I love you, I love you, I love you"(as you think of what you actually love) and then "I love myself". It is important to actually feel some love or compassion. "I forgive you, I forgive you, I forgive you" (– as you think of Dad, Mum, the school bully or anyone who hurt you in the past) and then: "I forgive myself". Continue with this until a negative memory or dream comes to mind regardless of how recent, ancient or trivial a might be. You may recall an incident from the previous week, something from your early childhood or even your birth. Note what feeling the memory or dream brings out in you. Rate that feeling on a score of 1-10. (1 being care free 10 being the height of distress)

[2]

MEANING

Repeat the mantra again several times. Pause. Feel a sense of peace and allow your mind to clear. Ask yourself;" What amI doing to myself (e.g.in the areas of health, relationships, career or whatever) because of that memory/dream or the people involved in it and how is that connected with my issue or illness?" Perhaps you recall an incident from your early childhood which brought out in your feelings of guilt and you now realize that habitually blaming yourself is creating stress or stopping you from attracting money or happiness.

[3]

MOVEMENT

Repeat the mantra again several times until you know how to move, change or erase the memory. Act it out in your mind – but this time forgive the parties involved especially yourself. Do whatever is indicated until you feel better. The purpose of all this is to release habitual negative feelings. The other people involved can also experience healing or relief telepathically.

This technique, if practiced daily can cleanse your energy, heal you and others, improve the atmosphere in a premises, activate the Law of Attraction in your favor and help you to achieve your goals.

Repeating the mantra, even without the three M's

several times a day can keep you in a good mood and your energy pure. However, if you don't set a reminder you may forget to do it so associate it with something you see quite often like a door or shoes. Say to yourself "Every time I see e.g. shoes, I will repeat the mantra".

Now that you understand the need for these changes in yourself it will also be necessary for you to act in accordance with your words. Constantly trying to get the better of others, always having to win the argument, being unkind to yourself or others, criticizing, manipulating, controlling, judging, or acting as if you are different from others because of social status, race, gender, age, color or creed will not help the process. We are all aspects of God's energy – temporarily encased in a human body. Good health and wellbeing depends on keeping your energy pure.

THE LIGHTHOUSE : HEALING LABORATORY

Working with this technique, which is also known as the 'Television Room' and the 'Workshop of the Mind' is more easily done with the aid of a therapist or a friend who can put you into a relaxed, meditative state using the Four-Minute Meditation or repeating a mantra. Think about what you choose to heal, change or improve in your life. Now imagine yourself inside a cylindrical tower or a pyramid. Furnish it any way you like. See three large computer screens on the wall in front of you to illustrate past, present and future, a full-length x-ray mirror to allow you to see inside the body and a shower unit to spiritually cleanse you or another of negative energy or entities. There are four doors with signs over them marked; (1) 'Exit', (2) 'Guides', (3) 'Others' and (4) 'Portal'. These can be used for contacting your Spirit Guides, confronting parents and others, sending unwanted entities and negative energy into other dimensions and so on. A vent in the wall like a laundry chute can take away your clothes (representing old attitudes) as you undress and spiritually cleanse yourself in the shower. If you choose to use the '3.M's' then screen No. 1 allows you to see images from the past (memories), No. 2 the effect of such memories in present time and No. 3 possible future outcomes. The Guides can be called in to help you heal these memories and the portal can be used to send negative energies and entities into other dimensions.

Much can be said about using these devices and facilities and you can read more about them in the e-book. Let us, with the space we have available focus on one such use. Your dream e.g. might highlight the difficulties you are having as a result of your father's perceived neglect. Call him, (whether dead or alive) in through door No, 3. Confront him, tell him how you feel about these issues and equally as important let him explain what he did or failed to do. You may be surprised at what you learn. End by expressing acceptance and eventual forgiveness. Doing this on a regular basis, in addition to all the other benefits can help develop your clairvoyance and channeling.

23

THE SECRET OF SUCCESS

Is it possible to change ones personality? Your personality is simply a collection of ideas, belief systems or opinions that you hold about yourself, other people or the World. For example; 'The World is a dangerous place. Men are not to be trusted. I am small and vulnerable – especially by being female", and so on. To relieve stress and heal or avoid illness all you need do is release such old, unhealthy notions. When you read the four Control Dramas, your first reaction might be; "I am none of the above". Try asking your friends what dramas you act out. Until you accept the darker 'shadow side' of your personality, you cannot plot a course to your Real Self. Acknowledge the extent to which you have subscribed to each or all of the personality types or Control Dramas.

Are you: e.g. 80% a Critic and 40% an Aloof? Can you connect your personality with your chronic illness, relationship difficulties or financial situation?

What Control Dramas did your father and mother use and how have you copied them or gone the opposite way?

List the ways in which you act out your Dramas and every day act out of character in at least one way.

The book, 'The Strange Case of Dr. Jekyll and Mr. Hyde' was inspired by a dream. The author Robert Louis Stephenson dreamt of how the good Dr. Jekyll takes a potion which releases his 'alter-ego' – the despicable Mr. Hyde who wreaks havoc with his life and eventually bring on his death.

Although it was a work of fiction, the story illustrates how the negative side of our personalities can bring trouble and illness – unless we decide to change.

In the Catholic school I attended, we were taught that a Devil exists who follows you around putting negative thoughts in your head and keeping you from getting closer to God. However, in all my dealing with this and other dimensions I never came across this 'Prince of Darkness' – only the darkness in ourselves called the 'Shadow Self'. Certainly, the latter keeps you from God or the idealism of your Real Self. Yes, he would qualify for a title – perhaps 'Father of Fear' would be appropriate. He is driven by fear and from that fear comes, hate, anger, greed, guilt, envy and every other darkness. Every negative thought, emotion and decision you make has its basis in fear. Every positive thought, emotion and decision has its basis in love and from that love comes compassion, acceptance, forgiveness and so on. In the words of the poem (at the back of the book):

'You are your own Devil. You are your own God.

You fashioned the pathways your footsteps have trod.'

So, is there a Devil after all – now called the Shadow Self and if so, should you put a stop to his career? If you want the future to change, if you want to heal yourself or someone else, if you want to attract better 'luck, happiness and abundance, you must first find your own devil (that aspect of you that holds you back) and change it.

But how can you do that? Ester and Jerry Hicks, authors of 'Ask and it is Given' recommended a 'step by step' method of gradual change.

This involves (a) accepting where you are in terms of your habitual negative emotions in present time and then (b) practicing or acting out an alternative emotion even if that seems like a retrograde step. In other words if you are a 'victim type' allow yourself to feel and express anger for a while and notice the relief this brings from your usual 'Poor Me' stress. Having experienced this emotion for two or three weeks raise your consciousness to the next step and act as if you are more accepting and so on. Continue with this until you arrive at love. Negativity and the stress and illness it brings are just a bad habit. You can change it if you wish. This process can also appear in dreams as 'steps, step-pyramids, etc.'

To achieve health, happiness, wealth, 'luck' and success the first rule is; absolute acceptance of the self and others'. The same pair that gave us the 'steps' technique above left us with a definition of the State of Acceptance:

'If you can look at other people 'behaving badly' (in your opinion) and feel no desire to change or control them you are in the State of Acceptance'. This is a pre-requisite for getting what you ask for. Naturally, children need a measure of control but ask yourself how much time and energy you expend every day and even every hour mentally trying to control adults in your life. In addition to the stress this causes you it can also put up a wall energetically preventing your wishes coming true.

Decide which parent contributed most to the creation of the Control Dramas aspect of your Shadow Self. Practice the procedure for 'Cutting the Ties that 'Bind' as described by Phyllis Krystal, with that parent and begin to think and act 'outside the box'.

Write out, in as much detail as possible what you desire using 'empowering' phrases such as "I choose to have/be/do.........". Next elaborate, again precisely why you choose to achieve this. (The 'Inner Child' aspect of your sub-conscious mind responds and co-operates better if you describe the positive effect of getting what you want)

Do not write or think about what you don't want. Your desire must be unconditional – no ifs, buts or strings attached.

Most importantly, regularly re-enter a dream using

the technique described in Chapter 6 and, regardless of the subject matter of the dream change it around so that it has a happy ending with you experiencing what it feels like to have the health, happiness, wealth, 'luck' or success you have chosen. This can have the effect of sending a message to the Universe in the secret language of the soul what exactly it is you desire and from the Law of Attraction. Consider also formally ordering in writing what you choose to "do, have or be" from the universe. Your dreams will respond by making you aware of any unwanted or unforeseen consequences of getting what you want. "Be careful what you pray for".

I have helped many people get their wishes in this manner.

24

SPIRITUAL HEALING

How often have you held a sick child and wished that you could heal or at least relieve its pain? What you may not know is that the hands you use to hold can also be used to heal. We are all healers. It is a natural part of the body's immune and self-healing mechanism. For example, if you break your leg the doctor will simple clamp the two parts together. One side of the leg will send healing to the other which will receive it. The leg then knits together and heals. See your hands as channels of healing. The left side of the body is female, receptive and magnetic. So you can use the left hand, moving anti-clockwise to draw out negative energy from the ailing part or relevant chakra. This might take about 10-15 minutes so be patient. You can then infuse positive energy into the spot with the right hand moving clockwise. This usually takes less time. With practice, the process can be speeded up.

Usually, you heal yourself from the front of your body and others from the back. If you have a magnet (even a fridge magnet), hold it in the left (receiving) hand, and a clear quartz crystal (if available), in the right (sending) hand. This can speed up the process. Move the left hand over the chakra area or troubled part in small circles anti-clockwise i.e. up the body and to the left and around. When you have extracted enough negative energy hold the left hand out palm upwards. Visualize the negative energy leaving your hand. Now the right hand moves clockwise i.e. up the body and to the right and around over the troubled area. Kinesiology can help you to determine when enough negative energy has been drained and enough positive infused. Stop every 5 minutes, connect the fingers and ask; "Have I extracted enough negative energy from this spot?" If you get a "no" continue until you get a "yes".

IMPORTANT

If you or your child is ill consult a registered medical practitioner. This work should be considered complimentary rather than alternative.

SIMPLE HEALING TECHNIQUE

USING CRYSTAL & MAGNET

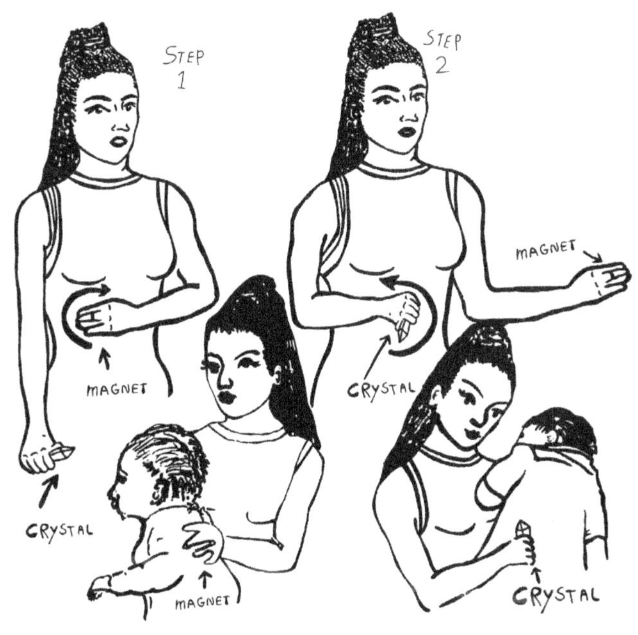

Fig. 7: Healing technique using crystal & magnet.

STEP 1.

Extract negative energy with the left hand (+magnet). This may initially require 10 minutes.

STEP 2.

Infuse positive energy with the right hand (+crystal). This may initially require 10 minutes.

You can also use these gifts and powers to awaken people to their spiritual and psychic potential. Sharing your abilities with another allows your soul to express itself. This can take you and the person you heal a step closer to alignment with the Real Self.

PREPARATIONS BEFORE HEALING

Before you begin the healing it is important that you get yourself into the right frame of mind. Healing or sending absent healing to someone if you are in a bad mood can be counter-productive so keep in mind the following:

(1) Cleanse your aura and the energy of the other party and premises by repeating the mantra; "I love you" (As you think of someone or something you love). "I'm happy" (Think of something that makes you smile). "I thank you" (Something for which you are grateful)."I forgive" (Someone who hurt you) "and am forgiven" (Someone you hurt). Visualize a ball of white or golden light slowly moving down

over your head and all the way down to your feet-penetrating deep into every bone, every muscle, nerve and cell – healing, cleansing, relaxing and re-energizing.

Command (use that word) anything negative to go into the ball. Bring the ball up your body, around your aura, the other party and the room. Send the ball up into the Universe.

(2) Imagine the other person is someone you actually love.

(3) Don't judge the other party, your ability or the process.

(4) Don't try too hard. Just let it flow with love.

(5) If any negative memory comes to mind or if you sense or feel a blockage in your own or the other party's body, visualize it being removed.

REMEMBER

THE INTENTION IS MORE IMPORTANT THAN THE TECHNIQUE

25

THE THREE STATES OF AWARENESS

Human beings are genetically programmed to evolve and improve. Each generation, consciously or subconsciously strives to be better and do better than the previous one. We know, intuitively, that the good qualities which were lacking in each of our parents are exactly what we need to develop in ourselves. For example, if your mother lacked patience and compassion, and your father was "not there for you", then an essential part of your Life Purpose will be to develop patience and compassion and support other people. Earth is like a reform school. We came here to become a better soul leaving the planet than we were coming in and in previous lives. This program is built into our genes.

Naturally, we are at various stages of this evolutionary process. For convenience, see these as states 3, 2, and 1 – the latter being advanced to such a degree that there is no longer any need to re-incarnate here.

According to the Spirit Guides, this mix of souls at various stages of development is unique to this planet and enables us to achieve rapid spiritual development if we choose to make the effort. More advanced souls can help those less advanced who seek help and answers. 'When the student is ready the teacher appears'. This three-step progression has been known by aware souls since the beginning of time. It has even appeared in fairy tales. We all remember from our childhood the story of Goldilocks and the Three Bears. Goldilocks wanders into the house of a family of bears and tries out their beds. Baby Bear's bed is too small. Daddy Bear's bed is not suitable either but Mammy's bed is exactly right. It is possible to see the awareness process using this analogy.

1.

THE BABY BEAR STAGE

This could also be called the Lower Karmic State. If you are at this level you may be emotionally immature and focused on basic human needs; survival, sex, competition, food, drink, sex, reproduction, etc. You are tribal and very competitive in groups. You may think of people in terms of "them and us". You demand instant gratification and get angry when these needs are not met. You take little responsibility for your health and expect the State to provide for all your needs. Spiritually, you are learning through drama and trauma, suffering, bad health, etc. You may have 'copied' the example of your parents to such an extent that you have 'become your mother and married your father'. Have you lost your spiritual identity in relationships? Do you need family approval to change or be different in any way? Do you make decisions based on fear?

2.

THE DADDY BEAR STAGE

This could be called the Upper Karmic State. This is a big improvement on the Baby Bear level. You are beginning to feel more responsible for your health and are, as a result, less stressed. You have developed some of your male aspects – individuality, the ability to manage and control, take responsibility for yourself and family and so on. You have developed your intellect and are comfortably in charge of your finances and career. You have learned some skill or ability in which you take pride. You base your decisions on confidence. On the negative side, perhaps you have become obsessed with work, house, possessions, money or family. Unfortunately, you may still feel the need to be top dog in work and relationships. Do you control yourself and others too much and show little regard for your 'softer', feminine aspects of intuition, caring, nurturing, etc?

3.

THE GOLDILOCKS STAGE

This, called the State of Dharma is the height of human spiritual evolution having the right balance of male and female aspects. You are now more aligned with your soul or Real Self. As a result health, wealth, miraculous good 'luck', success and everything you ask for naturally 'flows' to you. You have accepted and forgiven all who hurt you in the past and developed the good qualities that were lacking in your parents. You have learned to share yourself with the World and use your spiritual gifts with love, in the service of others. You are less competitive and understand that in order to win, you must help others to win. You are no longer trying to change or manipulate people using the Control Dramas. You have discovered love and happiness inside yourself. This allows you to love yourself and others. You no longer expect a partner to 'make you happy'. You now see relationships as opportunities for your soul or Higher Self to express itself. Your thoughts, emotions and decisions are more often based on love. You radiate a higher vibration and the Universe and other people respond in a positive manner. You feel at home in the Earth and the New Age. If God is Love, then you have become a little more god-like. The obsessions you had with your house, possessions, money, work and family has been replaced with spiritual non-attachment. You are amazed at the surge of miraculous healing and inspiration that flows through you. You have finally realized that you are God, or, at least an important aspect thereof. You have arrived.

It may sound like a fairy tale, but something on the lines of the above is the picture of life as indicated by

Dreams and Spirit Guides. Where are you in all of this? Most people are somewhere in-between these positions but you may be doing better than you think. Your spiritual development is not based on your intellect but rather on the extent to which you can learn to accept and love. Women – especially those who choose to be mothers, can make great spiritual progress – as can be seen from their dreams.

When you die, you, like everyone else on the Planet are not judged and assigned a place in the after- life. You simply gravitate to a level of existence that is consistent with your state of consciousness. It is an impersonal process and you find yourself living with like-minded souls on the same level of awareness as yourself. Whether that *feels* like heaven or hell depends on you.

In truth there is no hell. God has no need or desire to punish us, but he has imposed the Law of Attraction on us (ie. Karma & Dharma), which brings about perfect justice in the fullness of time.

You now have the knowledge to work with your Dreams. You can apply the techniques and methods that I have shared in this book to bring healing to every aspect of your life working with the Law of Attraction.

26

THE WISHING MAN

The cover image of this book was originally used on the first book, "Dreams, Secret Language of the Soul", published by Salmon Publishing in 1996. This image evokes a cosmic and spiritual perspective on our life on earth and emphasises the essential role of our dreams in connecting us to our wise inner guide : our Soul. Dreams are connected to our Soul or our Higher Self, and they also connect us to the Law of Attraction.

We see a naked man, he is looking down to earth and contemplating his next incarnation. He is sitting in the Halls of Learning between lives. We can see planet earth and stars in the distance.

Clothes in a dream represent attitudes. The "Naked

Man" in the cover image has dumped his negative attitudes. Now, he is ready to assume a new identity (clothes). The ultimate test of whether you are in the state of Acceptance or not is how comfortable you would be walking around naked! There is a stage in our spiritual development where it is common to dream about naked people. This is called the "naked man phase" of development, because it means that you have got rid of your negative old attitudes ie. your clothes. That means that, because you have been working on yourself, you have got rid of aspects of your old Self, you are ready to embrace a more positive way of being in alignment with your "Real Self", and your soul. How can we tell that we are closer to our "Real Self", or our soul? Being close to our soul brings feelings of joy, love and full self-expression through creativity and open communication. As we become more fully ourselves, rather than being ruled by the controlling and nanny-like "Shadow Self", we attract more aligned experiences and people into our lives.

You can use the "wishing man" image below as a focus when you write out your own wishes on the pages provided. You may wish to attract a loving partner, for example. Write and describe in detail all the qualities that you wish for in a partner. The subconscious mind responds to ritual, images and the written word. In keeping with the Law of Attraction, also consider how you yourself can express more of these qualities in your own daily life, remember : "like attracts like". If you want to attract a kind and loving man, consider how you yourself might express more kindness and love among the people in your life. Consider, for example, if you wish to attract a generous partner, how you might express a more abundant attitude. As you yourself come into alignment with these qualities that you would desire in a mate, you are already activating the Law of Attraction in your favour. Your dreams will show you how you may be blocking or limiting yourself. Your dreams may also indicate new possibilities for how you might develop your spiritual gifts and express more of your Real Self. Demonstrating an attitude of love and service, creates favourable conditions to bring the Law of Attraction into action in your life. Keep your "order", i.e. what you are asking for, in clear view so that you focus your creative imagination on achieving this.

One technique is to write your wishes in this book on the pages provided and then put the book under your pillow when you sleep. In this way, you will make a powerful impression on your subconscious mind, working with the Law of Attraction. A "Vision Board" is also a powerful tool. To create a Vision Board, write what you want on a large card or piece of paper and use inspiring images to illustrate and evoke the qualities, objects or person that you desire to attract into your life. Place the Vision Board in a prominent position so that you will see it everyday.

The language that you use is an important aspect of working with the Law of Attraction. Do not say " I want" or "I need". Instead, use empowering words:

"I choose to have a new relationship with a kind,

passionate, generous, fun loving man".

Also, put in a time-frame. For example, "within the next three months".

I CHOOSE

President Kennedy once made a speech:

"We choose to send a man to the moon within this decade..."

You can tell by the words he was using that he knew about Cosmic Ordering.

You *choose* to "have, do or be".

Write it out – sleep on it, or put your "vision board" where you can see it from your bed. Your dreams will immediately acknowledge your "Cosmic Order" and illustrate how you may be blocking yourself. For example, you may wish to have a relationship, but you are not creating space in your life to welcome a new partner. Your dreams will monitor the progress of your "order".

Focus is important. A lot of people wish for things and then ten minutes later wish for something different, contradicting perhaps their original wish. When you write out your Cosmic Order, you have made it clear what you want – and the subconscious mind respects that. The subconscious is very ritualistic. The fact that you have taken the time to write out clearly what you want makes an impression on your subconscious mind. When you illustrate your wish with images, and put it under your pillow or where you can see it this becomes even more powerful. Using a "Vision Board" increases the chances of your real Dreams coming true.

KEY STEPS FOR WORKING WITH THE LAW OF ATTRACTION

- Write our your "Cosmic Order" by writing in this book on the pages provided or by creating a Vision Board.
- Practice a Healing Mantra (see Chapter 10) and train yourself to re-direct negative thought patterns for a positive flow of energy in your life.
- Consciously seek to develop the positive qualities of Acceptance, Love and Forgiveness and to come into alignment with your Real Self.
- Begin to work with your spiritual gifts, as revealed in your dreams, and share these gifts with others.
- Use the Four Rules (see Chapter 3), and the Six Questions (Chapter 6) – to work with your dreams and gain insights into how you may be blocking yourself in manifesting your heart's desire.

Through developing an attitude of Love and Service, we can come into alignment with our Soul Purpose. Positive actions ensure the flow of positive energy and will activate the Law of Attraction in our favour. Our Dreams provide a way to access our inner visioning capacity and our powerful subconscious mind for guidance, healing and to attract what we want into our lives.

Fig.8: Cover Image "The Wishing Man"

27

MY COSMIC ORDER

My Law – Tieme Ranapiri

(KARMIC JOURNEY OF THE SOUL)

The sun may be clouded, yet ever the sun

will sweep on its course till the cycle is run.

And when into chaos the system is hurled

again shall the Builder reshape a new world.

Your path may be clouded, uncertain your goal.

Move on – for your orbit is fixed to your soul

And though it may lead into darkness of night

the torch of the Builder shall give it new light.

You were. You will be ! Know this while you are.

Your spirit has travelled both long and afar.

It came from the Source, to the Source it returns.

The spark that was lighted eternally burns.

It slept in a jewel. It leapt in a wave.

It roamed in the forest. It rose from the grave.

It took on strange garbs for long eons of years

and now in the soul of yourself it appears.

From body to body your spirit speeds on

It seeks a new form when the old one has gone

and the form that it finds is the fabric you wrought

on the loom of the mind from the fiber of thought.

As dew is drawn upwards, in rain to descend

your thoughts drift away and in destiny blend.

You cannot escape them, for petty or great,

or noble or evil they fashion your Fate.

Somewhere on some planet,

sometime and somehow

your life will reflect the thoughts of your Now.

My Law is unerring, no blood can atone-

The structure you built you will live in – alone.

From cycle to cycle, through time and through space

your lives and your longings will ever keep pace.

and all that you ask for, and all you desire

must come at your bidding as flame out of fire.

Once list' to that Voice and all tumult is done-

Your life is the Life of the Infinite One.

In the hurrying race you are conscious of pause

with love for the Purpose and love for the Cause.

You are your own Devil, you are your own God

You fashioned the pathways

your footsteps have trod.

And no one can save you from error or sin

until you have hark'd to the Spirit within.

ANONYMOUS – *Attributed to a Maori*

Further Reading

DREAMS – SECRET LANGUAGE OF THE SOUL, by George Rhatigan, Salmon Publishing (a division of Auburn House), 1996.

HEALING WITH DREAMS IN THE NEW AGE, by George Rhatigan, Amazon Kindle 2020.

CUTTING THE TIES THAT BIND WORKBOOK, by Phyllis Krystal, published by Samuel Weiser , 1995.

ZERO LIMITS, by Joe Vitale published by John Wiley and Sons, Inc., 2009.

Various books on Edgar Cayce, published by Virginia Beach, USA.

ASK AND IT IS GIVEN, by Ester & Gerry Hicks, published by Hay House, 2004.

THE SECRET, by Rhonda Byrne, published by Simon & Schuster, UK 2006.

CONVERSATIONS WITH GOD, by Neale Donald Walsch, Hodder & Stoughton 1998.

THE EMOTION CODE, by Dr. Bradley Nelson, Wellness Unmasked Publishing, Mesquite, Nevada, U.S.A., 2007.

INNER LIGHT RESOURCES, Inc. Rainbow Cards and Charts Series,

P.O. Box 82542, Tampa, Fl. 33682 U.S.

GO UP AND WORK WITH GOD, by Vianna Stibol, Rolling Thunder, U.S.A., 2002.

WINDOWS OF THE MIND, by G.M. Glaskin. Arrow Books, Ltd., 1975.

DREAMS YOUR MAGIC MIRROR: With Interpretations of Edgar Cayce. A.R.E. Press, 1995.

THE JOY OF STRESS, by Dr. Peter Hanson, Hanson Stress Management Organization, Canada, 1986.

REAL MAGIC by Dr. Wayne W. Dyer, Published by William Morrow Paperbacks, 2001.

THE CHANNELLED BOOKS of Brendan O'Callaghan, available on Amazon.

OTHER BOOKS BY THIS AUTHOR

"Dreams Secret Language of the Soul".

Auburn House 1996

'Healing with Dreams in the New Age',

on Amazon Kindle

FOR UPDATES ABOUT THIS WORK VISIT

www.healingwithdreams.com

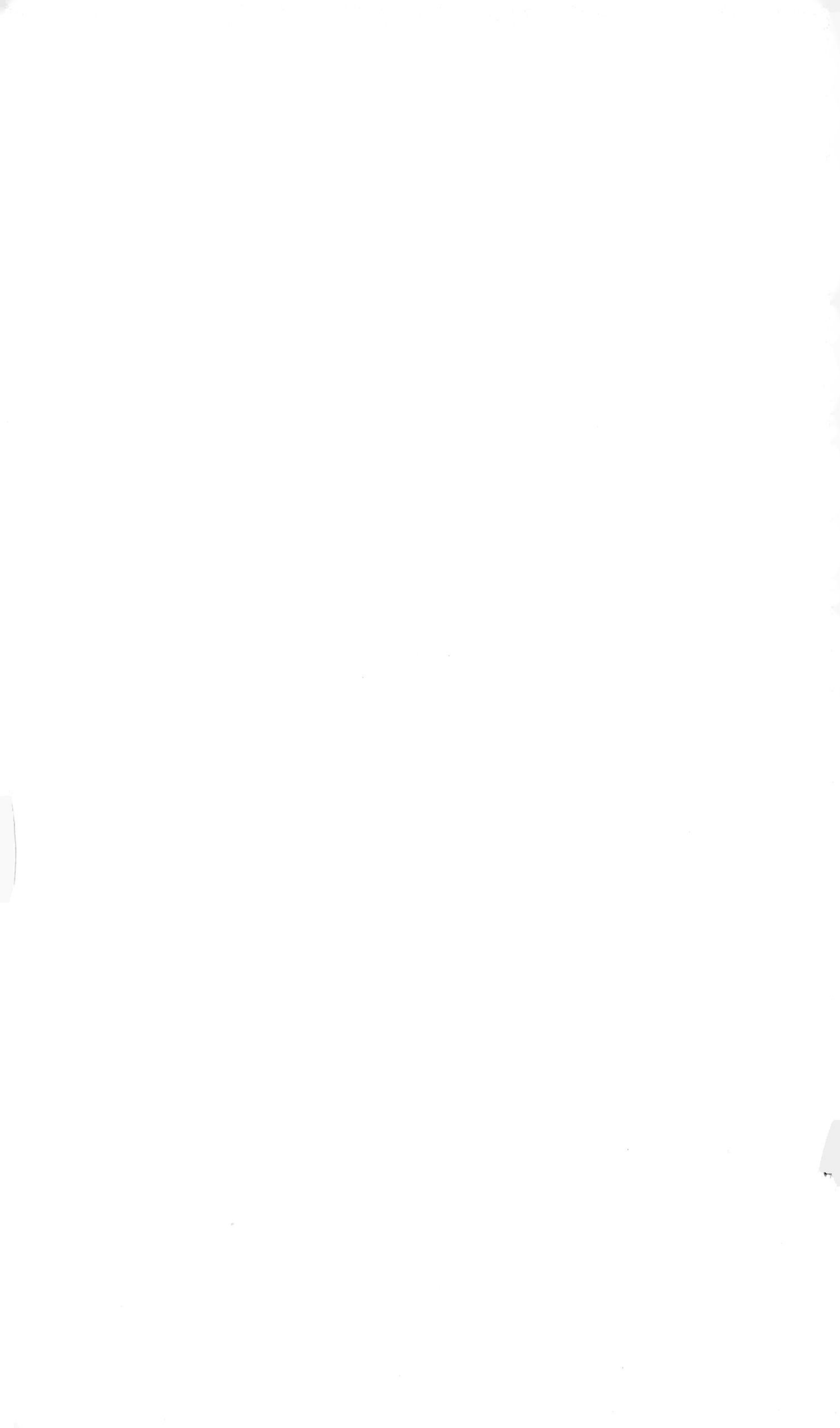

Printed in Great Britain
by Amazon

21364645R00203